on track ...

UFO

every album, every song

Richard James

sonicbondpublishing.com

Sonicbond Publishing Limited
www.sonicbondpublishing.co.uk
Email: info@sonicbondpublishing.co.uk

First Published in the United Kingdom 2021
First Published in the United States 2021

British Library Cataloguing in Publication Data:
A Catalogue record for this book is available from the British Library

Copyright Richard James 2021

ISBN 978-1-78952-073-6

Typeset in ITC Garamond & ITC Avant Garde
Printed and bound in England

Graphic design and typesetting: Full Moon Media

Thanks to ...

My thanks go to my wife, Alison, for – well – everything, and marking my homework! Multiple 'thanks-a-lot, ta's' to my best man and fellow frequent flyer, Mike Rawsthorne, who has been instrumental in commenting upon all the songs in this book. Also I am grateful to Stephen Lambe at Sonicbond Publishing whose help, advice, and encouragement has transformed 'I think I could do that' into 'Oooh, look, I've written a book'.

Would you like to write for Sonicbond Publishing?

We are mainly a music publisher, but we also occasionally publish in other genres including film and television. At Sonicbond Publishing we are always on the look-out for authors, particularly for our two main series, On Track and Decades.

Mixing fact with in depth analysis, the On Track series examines the entire recorded work of a particular musical artist or group. All genres are considered from easy listening and jazz to 60s soul to 90s pop, via rock and metal.

The Decades series singles out a particular decade in an artist or group's history and focuses on that decade in more detail than may be allowed in the On Track series.

While professional writing experience would, of course, be an advantage, the most important qualification is to have real enthusiasm and knowledge of your subject. First-time authors are welcomed, but the ability to write well in English is essential.

Sonicbond Publishing has distribution throughout Europe and North America, and all our books are also published in E-book form. Authors will be paid a royalty based on sales of their book. Further details about our books are available from www.sonicbondpublishing.com. To contact us, complete the contact form there or email info@sonicbondpublishing.co.uk

on track ...

UFO

Contents

Introduction

It's a Saturday afternoon in the spring of 1978, and I am sitting at my bedroom desk. On the floor lies an open copy of this week's *Sounds*, a weekly rock music newspaper, and in front of me, where my homework should be, is the monthly musicians' magazine *Beat Instrumental*. Sitting on the nearby windowsill is a small transistor radio with the volume set to 'uncomfortable'. Every Saturday afternoon was like this; my sixteen-year-old self had one all-encompassing passion, rock music, and I was about to get my weekly fix via the Alan Freeman Rock Show on Radio One.

This programme was like a cathedral to me. From its exciting introduction, (8.42 minutes into ELP's 'Karn Evil 9': 'Welcome back my friends to the show that never ends, we're so glad you could attend, come inside come inside'), to Freeman's dramatic voice, every song, every pronouncement sounded important. This was stuff I needed to hear, to really *listen* to, and Alan's wisdom would help me with my next investment. Because that's what records were, not just financially, but more importantly in finding your musical soul-mate in a seemingly ever-expanding universe of bands, styles, and sounds. A feature of the show was the final few seconds of Be Bop DeLuxe's 'Maid in Heaven', played as a potent introduction to what was to come. And then he played 'some UFO for you, alright?'.

The first time I heard a UFO song, I was stunned. I had read about them, the band with the German guitarist, but they hadn't come into full view yet. My initial immersion in rock's deep pool was via Status Quo, Black Sabbath, Rush, and Budgie. But I wasn't content with these bands; fabulous as they were I wanted something else, something that really *connected...*

It wasn't one of UFO's now-classic songs, or one of their very rare chart entries that first got my attention. My initial exposure was to 'Reasons Love' a track from their 1976 album *No Heavy Petting*, according to Alan. From my radio's small speaker emerged a bludgeoning electric guitar riff with pounding drums, heavy bass, and words that you could actually hear and understand, sung rather than shouted or screamed. And then there was the guitar solo, fierce, fast, and oh-so-melodic. Not rooted in the jazz/blues pentatonics of Sabbath's Iommi, or the country-tinged, spiky phrasing of Francis Rossi of Status Quo, this was superb playing with power, precision, passion, and unbelievable speed. I wanted more. A lot more.

Suddenly UFO was rising to the surface in time for me to purchase the taster EP teasing the release of *Obsession*. It contained three absolute belters, 'Only You Can Rock Me', 'Cherry' (both from the forthcoming album), and a longer track, 'Rock Bottom', from *Phenomenon*. It was this trio which exerted a gravitational pull on me. For an extra pound, plus postage and packing, I could own a promotional red plastic frisbee adorned with the UFO logo in the middle. When this finally arrived it turned out to be a complete waste of my Sunday farm job money. The disc contained no music and managed to ruin the stylus on the stereo system.

But from that point on my musical future with UFO was sealed. Every vinyl album was bought, then purchased in CD format, and then again in the 're-mastered/bonus tracks' era. My second ever gig was seeing the band at De Montfort Hall in Leicester on the *No Place To Run* tour. I've been to at least one show of every subsequent tour, and been a sucker for the merchandise stall. Live they never disappointed me, on record they sometimes did, but much less frequently than any other band.

As UFO's 50th anniversary/farewell tour draws to a close, and Phil Mogg, vocalist, chief lyricist, and only permanent member of the band has decided to retire, this is an appropriate time for an analysis of all of their studio albums. A separate chapter is included for the landmark live masterpiece *Strangers In The Night*, whilst other official live albums are treated as points of historical reference with minor comments.

UFO can be delineated by the many excellent guitarists who have passed through the ranks and Mick Bolton. Apologies to fans of Mr B but his playing just makes my teeth itch. Each period of the band has its devotees, with the possible exception of *Misdemeanor*, (although there may even be some 'Hair Metal' enthusiasts out there who rate that album above all others, as unlikely as it sounds), and throughout the book, I aim to be as fair as possible. Every album has its highs and lows, and these are reflected in both UFO's great and not so good contributions to rock's rich tapestry.

When I'm drawn to a song it's because it sounds original, has integrity, shows creativity, and carries emotional weight. Equally, spades will be called spades. These are the principles I have adhered to when writing this book, and my aim is to be as subjectively objective, or maybe the opposite, as possible. The opinions given are entirely my own, as are any mistakes that may filter through.

All the albums reviewed here are based upon listening to the latest CD versions available. Until 1990 I collected vinyl and, up to that date, the reviews reflect the side one and two divisions in sequencing where appropriate. After 1990 I became a CD listener (*Strangers* was my first purchase of the new medium) and the distinction between sides no longer mattered.

Writing this has been (mostly) a labour of love for a band that has provided a soundtrack to my life to date, and whose music will stay with me for as long as my ears and memory continue to function adequately. Strap yourself in... we're off on a rockin' ride...

UFO 1

Personnel:
Phil Mogg: vocals
Michael Bolton: guitars
Pete Way: bass
Andy Parker: drums
Recorded at Jackson Studios, Rickmansworth, Hertfordshire
Produced by Guy Fletcher and Doug Flett
Released on the Beacon label: October 1970
Highest chart places: Did not chart

In the autumn of 1970, the beginnings of a legendary band emerged onto the nascent heavy rock scene. As was the fashion of the time some introductory notes for potential purchasers were included on the album sleeve...

...they were young, probably not long out of school, and still experimenting with sound. Although they were quite accomplished musicians, the boys, Mick Bolton, 20, lead guitar; Pete Way, 19, bass guitar; Andy Parker, 18, drums; and Phil Mogg, 19, singer, were still having some difficulty co-coordinating ... Now we consider them to be together enough for us to release a first album. Many of the tracks are written between them and are a musical expression of their innocence and thoughts of the world we live in. We all hope you enjoy it as much as the boys did making it.

The album cover was a cheap and cheerless affair. Four disembodied egg-like globes with open 'mouths' float against a starry black sky backdrop. The band's logo and album title in white and grey are typical of the time. On the rear, a larger version of the same logo and title is shown above the list of songs. On the inside of the CD insert is a double-page photo of the group's heads against a black background, from left to right its Way, Bolton, Parker and Mogg.

Listening to this album for the first time in many years it's still hard to believe that three-quarters of the line-up on this first record would go on to become the core of a classic rock band. The essential elements, (Mogg's distinctive vocals, Way's energetic if rudimentary bass playing, and Parker's propulsive drumming), are all present and correct, but the trio is let down on two important fronts.

Bolton is fundamentally just another blues-rock guitarist and whilst his rhythm work is adequate, his solos rarely move beyond clichés. Virtually everything he plays has been executed better by other players, and he offers little beyond the uninspired regurgitation of bland blues phrasings. There is a lack of variation in his recorded guitar tone and he operates almost on a 'one sound suits all' setting.

More importantly, *UFO1* lacks quality songs. There is just about enough semi-decent material here to form an interesting EP but stretching what they've got over two sides of twelve-inch vinyl was a big ask. The album is of historical interest only, but if it hadn't existed quite probably what followed would never have happened. The most positive spin to put on this debut is that it's a first stepping-stone to future greatness. It's difficult to believe at times, but history bears me out. Just.

'Unidentified Flying Object' (Way, Mogg, Parker, Bolton)

This unassuming short instrumental opens with some gently picked guitar arpeggios over a wash of cymbals and a tasteful bass line, joined by a steady drum rhythm. Gradually the music increases in tempo and gains some urgency with a slow, distorted guitar melody featuring plenty of bluesy bends, along with some appropriately 'Sci-Fi' sound effects. The track gradually gets heavier before building to a power chord conclusion with more synthesiser noises to a fade.

It's pleasant enough without being anything other than mildly diverting, music to shave by if you like, but it's a curious choice for an opening track. A more appropriate title would be 'Un-involving Filler Object'.

'Boogie' (Way, Mogg, Parker, Bolton)

An angry guitar introduction leads to more bluesy noodlings over a steady 4/4 time hi-hat rhythm, which then drops into a rollicking 12/8 shuffle. The guitar riffs are strong here and anticipate both 'Give Her the Gun', and 'Doctor Doctor'. Unfortunately, Mogg's first vocal, although laconic in delivery, contains neither poetic nor subtle lyrics. Another problem with this underachieving song is that it constantly sits in the tonic key of A minor; there are no chord changes or separate sections to maintain interest over its four and a half minute duration.

A lengthy and staggeringly derivative guitar solo is followed by Mogg's reappearance, which is some form of relief even if his words appear to have been written whilst Bolton was playing. The song ends as it began with more blues phrasing, finally fading over the reprised shuffle rhythm.

'Boogie' would become an early stage favourite and is one of the stronger offerings in this poor first bunch. It was released as a single, and reached No. 30 in the German charts, setting the scene for the band's early popularity overseas.

'C'mon Everybody' (Cochran/Capeheart)

Third track in and UFO's first cover version starts with a combined assault of drums, bass, and heavily distorted guitar. Elsewhere in this book, I am critical of the band's decisions to record other artists' material when they possessed ample song-writing skills themselves. Here, however, this energetic remake of Eddie Cochran's rock' n 'roll classic is the best song on the album despite the dated production values, an example being the excessive use of echo on the title words, which spoils the inherent aggression of the track. Both guitar solos are short, sweet(ish), and appropriate, and the album has come to life with two strong numbers.

'C'mon Everybody' would remain part of the band's setlist during the early gigging days with Schenker and would make occasional reappearances later in the band's touring life.

'Shake It About' (Way, Mogg, Parker, Bolton)

Over an opening swing style walking bass line and drum rhythm, there is more bluesy noodling from Bolton, whose guitar probably thought *Oh no, not again* each time he plugged it in. Mogg's fine vocal style just about manages to cope with some awful lyrics, 'Little girl, you look so fine, with that body you gotta be mine'. The rhythm and tempo then pick up for the long and entirely predictable guitar solo. Mogg is back for another dubious verse, trading melodic phrases with Bolton who solos again before a new chord sequence underpins a long and impressive 'Shake' from Mogg as the song grinds to an end.

'(Come Away) Melinda' (Hellerman/Minkoff)

The sound of children playing foreshadows some softly wah-wah'd guitar chords with Mogg in a reflective mood. Here are the first true indications of his fine soulful style with real tone and emotion to his singing. The verse describes, in the first person, a young girl asking her father to look at something she has discovered. The chorus shifts to the father's perspective as he tries to protect her from the knowledge of a 'picture book' containing photos of her mother 'before the war'.

UFO would develop a long and proud tradition of high-quality ballads and, whilst this is a cover version, it is also an extremely persuasive interpretation of the original, first recorded by Harry Belafonte in 1963. Credit is due here to Parker's subdued, tasteful drumming, whilst Way is too prominent and busy in the mix. Some backwards recorded guitar is added as the song builds to a strong conclusion with Mogg's ghostly cries, and a 'reversed' piano sound, although no one is credited with playing this instrument. There are some gunshots as an unnecessary and obvious coda to this powerful track.

'Timothy' (Way, Mogg, Parker, Bolton)

This song begins with a lengthy and energetic up-tempo introduction which is similar in feel to 'C'mon Everybody'. This is then followed by 'call and response' verses between vocals and instrumentalists. After this reasonably promising start, Bolton goes for another aimless wander around the fretboard during which time it's better to listen to Way's frenetic bass playing supported by Parker's rapid drumming.

The 'breakdown' section (2.18) is of mild interest although lyrically it leaves a lot to be desired, 'Does he come from the sky? Does he come from the land? Does he come from the earth? Does he come from the sea? Timothy'. It's a throwback to the poorer side of psychedelia which is where it should have stayed. Then, in the same way that space abhors a vacuum, there is another guitar solo which, again, is unhampered by inspiration as Bolton replays blues phrasings already used on the album, followed by a brief power chord ending to the song.

'Follow You Home' (Way)

'Follow You Home' is based on a brisk 're-imagining' of The Kinks' 'You Really Got Me' riff played with a cleaner guitar sound. The refrain 'C'mon and see you in the morning' is catchy, but otherwise, the song remains mundane, with another pentatonic guitar assault on the listeners' boredom threshold. The track is a light, quick, pop-style number with a tight ending but little else to commend it, its saving grace being its brevity

'Treacle People' (Bolton)

It's back to the land of cod-psychedelia, with this slow pseudo-Beatles ballad. Bolton's sole solo composition does not fare well. Abysmal lyrics make their way effortlessly through the band's seemingly non-existent quality control system, 'I walked through the space, that wasn't really there, and when I reached the other side, I didn't really care'. Nor do we.

A guitar solo rooted in the major key feel of the song is of partial interest and is the first time that Bolton appears to have something original to contribute musically. After the solo, the line 'Everyone except for me' is another example of the potential of Mogg's voice, soulful with an edge, a rasp showing genuine emotion. The instrumental section is reprised with added studio modulation effects. 'Treacle People' is interesting only because new ideas are introduced and explored, but it is let down by truly terrible words

'Who Do You Love' (McDaniel)

Opening with another gentle guitar introduction with various 'coo-ings' from Mogg, subtle cymbal washes, and sparse drum fills, the band then come crashing in with a rhythm reminiscent of The Who. Lyrically it is best avoided amid the repeated 'Who do you love's. Then, of course, there's a predictable pentatonic blues solo, drenched in excessive reverb. It all sounds like an amateurish jam, a recorded rehearsal, with more dreadfully clichéd lyrics. Mogg's final refrain is, however, particularly impressive and it's moments like this that reveal the depth of talent waiting for the necessary German touch paper to ignite it.

The long instrumental sections show yet again how quickly Bolton could run out of ideas. A strong contender for the worst song on the album amidst some tough competition, it also lasts over seven *long* minutes. This cover version has no redeeming features aside from its mildly diverting introduction, and it reeks of filler to make up the album's running time.

'Evil' (Way)

The guitar introduction brings 'Lola' by The Kinks briefly to mind, and then the song descends into another mid-tempo blues-based number with more painful words, 'Heaven knows, but you're an evil child, drive me crazy you drive me wild'. Way's bass playing is so much better than his songwriting. Parker does his level best to keep the energy level up, but Bolton's one-sound-one-style solo comes in exactly when you would anticipate, and the soul is sapped again. The first verse is reprised, a go-to example of a lack of ideas, followed by yet another guitar solo as the song fades into well-deserved obscurity.

Non-Album Track
'Galactic Love' (Way, Mogg, Parker, Bolton)

Beginning with some suitably spacey 'Sci-Fi' effects, Parker's drumming propels the band into another sub-Who style chord progression which leads into yet another meandering number. Mogg's vocals have yet again had too much reverb applied to them. Bolton's solo is mercifully short and the opening verse and chorus are reprised before the song drags to a slow ending.

'Galactic Love' was released as a single in 1972, backed with 'Loving Cup', another impressive cover, this time of Paul Butterfield's blues song, taken from the band's third album.

U F O Two: Flying: One Hour Space Rock

Personnel:
Phil Mogg: vocals
Mick Bolton: guitar
Pete Way: bass
Andy Parker: drums
Recorded at Nova Studios, London
Produced by Milton Samuel
Released on the Beacon label: October 1971
Highest chart places: Did not chart

All five tracks on this opus are credited to all four band members. It's good of them to take collective responsibility for this protracted belch of a (very) long-player as *UFO Two: Flying: One Hour Space Rock* is almost entirely a turgid extension of all the problems that beset *UFO1*. And then some. There is more, a *lot* more, uninspiring, blues-based guitar playing, dull arrangements and three overly long songs, excessively so in the case of the title track. There is a minor improvement in the production; the level of reverberation added to the recording is noticeably reduced which leaves all the music sounding 'dryer' but this adds no polish to these particular musical droppings.

The cover was a painting of a naked alien figure flying towards the viewer accompanied, or pursued, by two blue UFOs. It looked like a failed sixth form art project. On the gatefold sleeve the lyrics were reprinted (which was not a wise decision), and only served to show how much the arrival of Michael Schenker would become a focal point and inspiration for the band's future success.

Bolton left the band in January 1972, his tenure being rounded off with a final album, *Live*, which confusingly has also been released with the titles *UFO Landed Japan*, *UFO Lands In Tokyo*, and *Live In Japan*, recorded and released exclusively in Japan in 1971. The rest of the world had to be patient until November 1972. It wasn't worth the wait. The first side was all cover versions ('C'mon Everybody', 'Who Do You Love', 'Loving Cup'), the second side all original material ('Prince Kajuku', 'The Coming Of Prince Kajuku', 'Boogie', 'Follow You Home'), with only 'C'mon Everybody' and 'Prince Kajuku' coming over well. The other strong studio song, 'Boogie' is, at ten minutes plus, far too long.

Flying is hard work; just ask an overweight buzzard. But this album, in particular, is a tough listen. Maybe it slides by better with recreational drugs or copious amounts of strong alcohol, but without such accessories, it's a serious contender for one of the worst listening experiences of my life. And I've heard amateur musical theatre companies in rehearsal.

'Silver Bird' (Way, Mogg, Parker, Bolton)

This starts with an upbeat bass and drum backing with a folky-style clean electric guitar melody over which Mogg's restrained vocals can just about be heard, both the guitar and bass being too far forward in the mix. The 'story', such as it is, describes the discovery of a landed UFO with a subsequent invitation from its inhabitant to take the narrator away from Earth, a suggestion that is accepted.

The rock feel is turned up and the song crashes into a loose, interminable blues instrumental which shows absolutely no development from *UFO1*, followed by a return to the verse structure. Then it's instrumental time again with Bolton demonstrating just how boring a guitar can be when in the wrong hands. At 4.10 a lengthy calmer section arrives featuring a wah-wah pedal solo which bounces in-between the stereo channels and builds with plenty of syncopated power chords over an increasingly energetic rhythm section before it all crashes to a typical early 1970s drawn out, power-chord ending.

'Star Storm' (Way, Mogg, Parker, Bolton)

'Star Storm' opens with a *long* introduction featuring a mixture of atmospheric guitar, percussion effects and a pulsing bass line until a mildly interesting light-funk guitar riff takes over at 2.10, and Mogg's distinctive vocals do their best with the car-crash lyrics which mix the interstellar with the interpersonal. A form of relief is on hand as Bolton solos briefly into the second verse and on it goes; verse and solo moving into an *extensive* instrumental section with Bolton's new toy, a delay pedal, being used extensively alongside the wah-wah. But his playing is all blues, blues, boring blues set against a monotonous backing. By this point, Mogg is probably in the pub writing the next verse. What interest there was is quickly lost.

At some point halfway through the track (it's difficult to be precise as I may have dozed off), Parker stops playing leaving Bolton and Way dithering away, echoes, wah-wah and reverb all over the place. This may be a symbolic voyage through space and time, but for those of us left behind it's the musical equivalent of a wet weekend in a broken-down Camper Van on an industrial estate just outside Stoke.

At 11.15, out of nowhere, a bizarre folk melody with a clean guitar tone emerges over a simple bass motif and Parker picks up his sticks again. Bolton quickly shakes off any notion of recent invention, retreating back to the safety of the 'B' word. At 13.20 the sound suddenly becomes heavier again with a basic guitar riff grinding away, and the tempo and the blues clichés gather pace as the music grinds into a new section of distorted power chords at 14.35 sounding like an outtake from the first Queen album.

Whereas Brian May would have fashioned this idea into something worthwhile and interesting, Bolton isn't going to let originality get in the way of his playing. So it's back on with his blues-trousers, whilst Parker starts to hit all of his kit hard and fast. Eventually, the original riff returns signalling both the fact that Mogg has returned from the pub, and that the song's coda can't be too far away. At least one of these statements is true and the track ends crisply, but it's still over eighteen minutes of your life you won't see again.

'Prince Kajuku' (Way, Mogg, Parker, Bolton)

A muted, wah-wah flavoured, arpeggiated guitar leads into a really good if simplistic overdriven riff and the first evidence of a recognisable UFO groove as Way and Parker pick up the rhythm and move together seamlessly. Mogg's vocals are again let down by some desperately poor pseudo-psychedelic lyrics, which actually describe the band's van driver, whose appearance apparently resembled that of a Zulu warrior. This is the first time the youthful energy of *UFO1* has been recaptured and it's a shame that it's taken nearly half an hour to get to this point. Bolton's solo is predictably mediocre but given what's gone before this noisy surprise of a song lifts the album with its vitality and concise delivery.

'Prince Kajuku', backed with 'The Coming of Prince Kajuku', was released as a single and made it to 26 in the German charts. Reflecting UFO's lack of popularity in their home country it failed to trouble the British charts.

'The Coming of Prince Kajuku' (Way, Mogg, Parker, Bolton)

This is another oddity, reminiscent of the attention-dodging instrumental which opened *UFO1*. After some restrained but not completely in tune chord work, another two-note bass motif allows Bolton to doodle away whilst the Gods of Inspiration gather over other guitarists. Parker's crisp drumming brings a Beatles 'Get Back' rhythmic feel to the music, but this track isn't going anywhere. Bolton starts to fiddle around with a dull chord progression, and then Way goes off for another lengthy wander around the fretboard. Gradually more layers of musical aggression are brought in as the bass drops an octave and provides some much-needed power as the music crashes to a tight ending. But what purpose has it served? 'The Coming of Prince Kajuku' is either a song waiting to be developed further or something thrown together to push the album's running time closer to its required titular level.

'Flying' (Way, Mogg, Parker, Bolton)

'Flying' is the longest track UFO would ever record and, sadly, the album's (partial) title track just drones on and on, seemingly without an end in sight. Various moods are elicited, then disposed of, and somewhere in this aural equivalent of Chinese water torture, there are some half-decent ideas which may have become interesting *short* songs given work. But it was not to be.

And so it begins. After some echo-heavy guitar effects, a derivative chord progression is established with Bolton possibly imagining he is being both tasteful and inventive. He isn't, and isn't. Mogg's subdued vocals grow, and lyrically it's as embarrassing as anything else on this album, but he does at least show control, phrasing and dynamic strength over the first five verses. Then inevitably it's time for a Bolton solo section (you know what you're going to hear even before it happens), which is followed by a return to Mogg and his next rambling five verses. There then follows a lengthy, and boy do I mean *lengthy*, instrumental section over which some very rudimentary ideas, far too reliant upon wah-wah and reverb effects, are strung out.

This is the first time I have listened to this album since the late 1970s when it was purchased, *had* to be purchased, because it was *early* UFO. I can still remember the deep disappointment upon discovering that this version of the band had virtually none of the features of the UFO that had captured me. 'Dull' doesn't begin to cover this music, and whilst writing this I am searching for moments, fragments, anything of worth to mention but there is very little here that you should allow your ears near. You could cast yourself Germany-wards and hear what the younger Schenker was up to with his brother's band, Scorpions, on their 1972 debut album *Lonesome Crow*. It's not much better, but at least it's not this.

At 12.25 the tempo suddenly cranks up with a different riff leading into a new vocal from Mogg, but interest is again short-lived as Bolton is back to plagiarising himself. This section could have had some merits as a song in its own right, but it's hidden away in this morass of improvisation and paucity of invention. Mogg sounds as if he's making the words up on the spot. Perhaps he is. Without warning or reason the music then moves into waltz time (3/4) and at 16.52 slows in tempo moving back into the default 4/4 setting.

This new sound world isn't going to hold Bolton back from committing more musical atrocities and, lo, it came to pass that the wah-wah and delay pedals were again deployed in a futile attempt to generate drama. And drama there was none. And the listener said unto himself 'Why is this happening to my ears? Make it stop.' And yet on it grinds, the tempo flat-lining to nothing as Way and Parker just...disappear.

Hang on I've just heard a chicken! I'm sure I have just heard a chicken. I am not making this up. At 19.48 it's either a chicken or I have genuinely lost it listening to this stodgy quagmire. I've reset the disc. Yes, that is, without doubt, a chicken. 'Mein Gott', a teenage guitarist in Hanover may be thinking. To the best of my knowledge, this is the first and last time a chicken has featured in rock music. The chicken also gets bored because Bolton is on his own now, with wah-wah, distortion, delay, and agonised string bends all over the place. Way and Parker return to the studio, maybe having enjoyed a very recent drumstick-style snack, and another five verses take hold. By this point, even the stereo is begging to be turned off...

Eventually of course 'Flying' does finish, and relief isn't a big enough word. The 'song' concludes with some unusual sound effects, some backwards recorded spoken words taken from Kipling's' 'Gunga Din', and a slowed down phrase 'Yes we know, it's all been done before, before, before'. No, I don't know why either.

Phenomenon

Personnel:
Phil Mogg: vocals
Michael Schenker: guitars
Pete Way: bass
Andy Parker: drums
Recorded at Morgan Studios, London
Produced by Leo Lyons
Released on the Chrysalis label: May 1974
Highest chart places: USA: 202, UK: Did not chart

In 1974, armed with a new record deal, management and guitarist, UFO finally took flight. The departure of Mick Bolton had been followed by brief periods with Larry Wallis (February to October 1972), and Bernie Marsden (November 1972 to June 1973), with the band recruiting *wunderkind* Michael Schenker from Scorpions whilst on tour in Germany. To doctor (doctor) a phrase; what a difference a guitarist makes.

From the very first track, it's hard to believe that three-quarters of this 'new' band were responsible for the exploratory, psychedelic, bluesy music of their first three records. *Phenomenon*'s songs are just *so* much better, well structured, and highly melodic. The production is clear, rocky, and direct, and the guitar playing appears to have emanated from a distant galaxy, or Hanover to be more precise.

Even the album cover, the first of many for the band by design group Hipgnosis, marked a superior change of focus and direction. The front image of a suburban couple attempting to fake a photograph of a UFO sighting outside their home is a welcome and intriguing departure. The back cover featured a large black and white image of the band, naked from the waist up, and a small inset of the real 'fake' photo, along with the song titles and credits.

This is the first 'true' UFO album. It features strong vocal performances, impassioned, poetic lyrics and, for the first time, some excellent original songs. Schenker's arrival and creative chemistry with Mogg, along with his soloing prowess, immediately makes a substantial and lasting break with the band's past. There would be no turning back from this point.

Phenomenon has an emphasis on dynamics and texture, with memorable riffs and two outright rock anthems rubbing shoulders with more reflective acoustic moments. It's fair to say the album has many softer sounding songs and, yes, four ballads may be overdoing it. But that is to miss the point. The essential elements of a classic band are in the chemistry between the players and the quality of the songs they produce. In this regard the new UFO delivered.

Phenomenon is not without its faults, but it still stands up as both a fine album in its own right and as a marker for the direction in which the band were headed. Their future would be in expertly crafted songs, full of melody and skilful arrangements. Song lyrics would be delivered with a soulful voice, and a rock-hard rhythm section quite capable of turning it all the way up or dialling in subtlety. Add to this a guitarist who combined killer riffs with breathtaking solos and it's a potent combination. Better was to come, more cohesion was on the horizon, and the album's sequencing is questionable, but all in all, this 'debut' is a strong statement of intent.

In 2019 Chrysalis released a 3CD deluxe package of the album. CD1 contained the original album, whilst the second disc included some interesting obscurities: 'Sixteen' (demo), 'Oh My' (demo), 'Give Her The Gun' (non-album single A-side), 'Sweet Little Thing' (non-album single B-side), 'Sixteen', 'Doctor Doctor' (single edit), 'Rock Bottom' (single edit), 'Doctor Doctor' (mono single edit), 'Oh My' (instrumental run-through), 'Sixteen' (instrumental), 'Doctor Doctor' (take two instrumental), 'Rock Bottom' (double-tracked vocal), 'Time On My Hands' (work-in-progress version, alternate lyrics, no guitar solo), 'Built For Comfort' (master with full vocal), 'Lipstick Application' ('Lipstick Traces' backing track), and 'D minor, G minor' ('Queen Of The Deep' master, full vocal, full ending).

It is the third disc which is the real find in this well-presented package. It captures UFO live at the Electric Ballroom, Atlanta, Georgia on 5 November 1974. The band delivers blinding versions of: 'Oh My', 'Doctor Doctor', 'Built For Comfort', 'Give Her The Gun', a cover of John Lennon's 1969 song 'Cold Turkey', 'Space Child', 'Rock Bottom', 'Prince Kajuku'

Nowadays running orders can be manipulated with ease compared to the dark ages of the record player and cassette recorder. To create a more *Phenomenon*al experience, try the following: 'Give Her The Gun', 'Crystal Light', 'Oh My', 'Space Child', 'Queen Of The Deep', 'Doctor Doctor', 'Time On My Hands', 'Sixteen', 'Lipstick Traces', 'Rock Bottom'

'Too Young To No' (Way/Mogg)
A slinky guitar introduction slides into a mid-tempo groover with a jaunty lead melody overlaid on top. The first song of the new era is not as ear-catching as the more powerful numbers on the album, and whilst the chorus is memorable 'Too Young To No' is hardly essential listening. It's pleasant enough in a light rock/hard pop fashion, and Schenker gets plenty of opportunity to show off his fretboard skills, but Mogg's lyrics (concerning a man's desire for a teenage girl) are nothing special.

Schenker's contribution, whilst establishing his trademark melodic style, sounds like the guitarist is treading water rather than thrusting forwards. The repeated choruses lead to the coda section, which has extra drive to it as the song comes to a sudden stop. Welcome to the future…

'Crystal Light' (Schenker/Mogg)

An acoustic guitar pattern opens this song and signals an abrupt change of mood. 'Crystal Light' is the first ballad, almost folky in style, but it steers well away from cliché. The backing is a well-balanced mix of guitar, bass and drums, with Mogg's evocative lyrics describing life on the open road on a cold night, 'Winter mists along the coast, city lights closed down'. His heartfelt delivery matches the song's arrangement to a tee. Both the verse and chorus feature uncredited backing vocals, presumably by the rest of the band, and they are not the high point of this song. The solo after the second chorus has a lonesome and constantly melodic quality to it, perfectly matching the lyrical pictures painted. After the final chorus, the track closes with more subtle guitar arpeggios.

'Doctor Doctor' (Schenker/Mogg)

If there's one song any rock fan will associate with UFO, this is it. The introduction is again subtle with the simple guitar fills sounding like a seagull's cry that is soon displaced by the heavy guitar, bass and drums onslaught. 'Doctor Doctor' then launches into a shuffle rhythm which never lets up. In lesser hands, this would be nothing more than a good-time boogie number, but the combination of Schenker's harmonised phrasing and Mogg's vocals lift what could become routine into the iconic.

The song's slight story of a man requiring medical attention after a romantic rendezvous gone wrong is nothing special, although Mogg's syncopated phrasing of the line, 'That's not a situation, for a ner-ner-vous boy' showcases the singer's confident style. The relative simplicity of the composition lends it a greater urgency with its infectious repetition and spontaneous feel and subsequent classic status in the UFO discography. The refrain 'Livin' lovin', I'm on the run, so far away from you' would rebound from concert hall walls the world over for decades to come. There isn't a specific guitar solo as such; an instrumental chord progression appears with a return to the harmonised guitars and the eventual fade.

'Doctor Doctor' was released as a single at the time and failed to chart, but a live version from *Strangers In The Night* reached Number 35.

'Space Child' (Schenker/Mogg)

The third consecutive number to start with a gently picked introduction, 'Space Child' is another 'folk-ballad', this time in slow 6/8 time. Mogg's vocals soar, especially with the emotive phrase 'Fly on over' just prior to the guitar solo. Here is a singer with real range, power, control and soul to his voice. Schenker's solo, featuring a smoother tone, is never flashy or over-indulgent. He wrings every ounce of emotion from his guitar, just building and building whilst Parker's sparse jazz-inflected drumming keeps the song moving forward. After the mesmerising solo Mogg returns for a brief verse before 'Space Child' finishes as it began, with an added brief guitar flourish.

'Rock Bottom' (Schenker/Mogg)

This timeless classic opens with not only the best Schenker riff but the greatest guitar riff ever written. It will never win any 'Top Riff' awards, where commercially more successful songs from bigger bands have cornered the market, but 'Rock Bottom' knocks them all out of the park. It's not easy to play, but its complexity is not in the 'clever-for-clever's-sake' style of prog-rock bands. Combined with the insistent 'Rock bottom' chorus refrain it makes for an irresistible combination.

This is the closest UFO would come to outright heavy metal, and the song is a monumental piece of work, the longest track on the album, and a magnificent showcase for Schenker's prowess. Full of energy and drive, the double-tracked riff underpins the song, but there is more than just metal to the track; Mogg's intelligent lyrics concern ageing and death, and are a sure sign of the heights he was capable of scaling. His 'rock' tone of singing is just as compelling as the more soulful voice he reserves for the ballads.

After a second verse and chorus, there is a half-tempo bridge section and then we're off to the races as Schenker solos as if his life depended upon it. It's immense, shrill in tone but never outstays its welcome. There's phrasing, vibrato, and a great sense of melody, and as he ups the intensity, the notes just cascade from his guitar, becoming faster and faster without ever losing control.

Utilising the 'Where do we go from here?' bridge chord sequence for his final breathtaking pyrotechnics, the song moves to an instrumental-only version of the chorus before Mogg returns for the third verse which, disappointingly, is just a re-run of the first verse. There is a final chorus and then an aggressive coda of power-chords, under which Way scurries up the fretboard before the stabbed finish. Schenker was still a teenager when he wrote and recorded this, his contribution is utterly astonishing for his years, and his playing marks him out as a massive and completely individual talent.

'Oh My' (Schenker/Mogg/Way/Parker)

This sprightly rocker is based around a Status Quo-like boogie rhythm with a jaunty lead guitar melody, and the band bristles with confidence and direction. Mogg's lyrics present a young man brimming with swagger, although his words are amateurish until the self-aware refrain, 'Oh my, oh how the times have changed', over an unexpected rhythmic syncopation. The vocals are interspersed with inventive lead fills whilst relentless bass and muscular drumming drive the track along. During the instrumental the guitar melody soars over a rising chord progression, reaching a plateau, before dropping back down into the original structure. The song pauses, restarts, and fades after another refrain.

'Time On My Hands' (Schenker/Mogg)

Beginning with an acoustic guitar 'Time On My Hands' is from the same stable as 'Crystal Light' and 'Space Child', the blend of subtle guitar, bass and light drums being highly effective. Mogg's vocals weave their spell especially in the chorus, 'I've got time on my hands, been drinkin' with a sailor boy, been tryin' hard to understand, lines here in my hand'. After the third verse, Schenker's solo again emphasises melody and context over the number of notes he could play, with his sustained tone raising the song to a higher level. There is a repeat of the chorus and the music begins to fade with Mogg's haunting repeated refrain 'I'm feeling blue again' over a play-out of the acoustic guitar introduction.

'Built For Comfort' (Dixon)

I have an issue with a band with the collective song-writing talents of Mogg, Schenker and Way deciding to record cover versions. Whilst 'Built For Comfort' is a muscular re-interpretation of a blues standard the question remains, *Why is it on this album?* Mogg is in good emotive voice, the band lock into a steady groove, and Schenker shines in a blues setting even though the genre is not his natural musical home, but the inclusion of this song is a wasted opportunity.

Was there a shortage of original songs deemed good enough to include? Listening to the non-album single 'Give Her The Gun' gives the lie to that argument, and even 'Sixteen', the 'bonus' track which emerged on the 2007 re-mastered CD, is more deserving than this. This number should be filed under 'Seemed like a good idea at the time', and stronger subsequent UFO albums would not contain reinterpretations of other artists' work.

'Lipstick Traces' (Schenker)

'Lipstick Traces' is a pretty instrumental in a romantic vein with echoes of The Shadows in its composition and execution. Schenker credits Hank Marvin as an early influence on his playing and here his cleaner sounding guitar tone is restrained, underpinned by acoustic guitar, simple bass and sparse drums in 6/8 time. There is some pleasing harmony work towards the end and it sounds like the sort of tune you could take home to meet your mother, but another song would have been preferable. 'Lipstick Traces' has a strong melodic core and is a short diversionary showcase from what's gone before, but to include it as a fully-fledged album track wasn't the band's best decision.

'Queen Of The Deep' (Schenker/Mogg)

A fifth quietly picked guitar opening, with Mogg's mysterious lyrics and soulful delivery, 'Heaven help the lucky ones, heaven help you', creating the impression of a big ballad to end the album. Then the overdriven guitar, bass and drums crash in and we're into a heavy, blues-tinged number which burns away at the end of *Phenomenon* like a spiteful fire.

Schenker opts for a shrill, agitated solo tone as the instrumental section begins with Way's bass prominent as a counterpoint to the German's manic creativity. A sudden flurry of repeated notes indicates both the end of the instrumental and also that the band had no idea how to join the solo section to a reprise of the verse. So instead, the song just stops and starts afresh. A blistering chord riff sends the track into a quick fade and then it's all over. 'Queen Of The Deep' is an overlooked gem but one that needed further development to transform it into the epic that UFO may have been seeking as the final track.

Non-Album Tracks
'Give Her The Gun' (Schenker/Mogg)
Released as a single before *Phenomenon* emerged, it's a mystery why 'Give Her The Gun' did not make it onto, or even open, the album. As a call to arms, it has everything UFO do so well.

    A rolling minor triad riff with added guitar fills gathers power as the song moves into a shuffle rhythm, and immediately it is superior to at least three tracks on the album. Mogg's refrain 'I don't know why she brings me on' again shows his confidence as a vocalist. It may have been felt that 'Give Her The Gun' was too close in style to 'Doctor Doctor' but, aside from the 12/8 time signature and similar medium tempo, there is much more going on here than in its more famous cousin. The song is one of Mogg's odes to the joys of fast driving and the band sound on fire throughout, the pace never letting up until the abrupt ending.

'Sweet Little Thing' (Way/Mogg)
A sub-Status Quo chugging rhythm and uninspired lyric prevent this predictable mid-paced stroll from rising above anything other than humdrum. This is a routine 'B-side' of a song with little going on to hold the attention despite some submerged-in-the-mix piano adding minor interest. Schenker's work is adequate enough but he is playing well within his capabilities, contributing some interesting Thin Lizzy style guitar harmonies before the chorus returns again. Just when you expect it to finish ... it carries on, and on, and on, coming eventually to another sudden stop.

'Sixteen' (UFO)
A pulsing bass line with sustained guitar fills builds into a funk-like introduction before a manic chord progression, with shades of The Who in its energy level and vocal line which gives 'Sixteen' more life. The song would have made a better B-side to 'Give Her The Gun', and could have made the cut for *Phenomenon*. This would, however, have meant losing one of the ballads which provide a welcome counterpoint to the sturm und drang of 'Rock Bottom' and 'Queen of the Deep.'

Force It

Personnel:
Phil Mogg: vocals
Michael Schenker: guitars
Pete Way: bass
Andy Parker: drums
Guest musicians:
Chick Churchill: keyboards
James Dewar: backing vocals
Recorded at Morgan Studios, London
'Let It Roll' and 'High Flyer' recorded at Wessex Sound Studios, engineered by
Mike Thompson
Produced by Leo Lyons
Engineered by Mike Bobak
Released on the Chrysalis label: July 1975
Highest chart places: USA: 71, UK: Did not chart

On *Force It* UFO finally hit their stride and became the fully-fledged hard rock band they had alluded to with *Phenomenon*. Five of the new album's songs would feature on *Strangers* and have, to varying extents, been stage favourites ever since. On *Force It* there is a single ballad with everything else being differing shades of the rock spectrum, ranging from all-out metallic thunder, good-time rock 'n' roll, multi-dynamic class, and their own version of epic.

The cover, another minor classic by Hipgnosis, depicted a semi-naked couple (Genesis P-Orridge and Cosey Fan Tutti who would go on to form industrial music group Throbbing Gristle), in a passionate embrace in a bathroom, the emphasis being on the wordplay of the title and the American word for tap. On the back cover, the 'faucet' theme was continued with four additional small individual photos of Mogg, Way, Schenker and Parker playing live. The front cover was considered too explicit by American distributors and the passionate pair was faded to ghostly outlines for the US market.

In 2007 *Force It* was re-issued as a remastered CD with previously unreleased live versions of 'Mother Mary', 'Out In The Streets', 'Shoot Shoot', 'Let It Roll', and 'This Kid's'. There was also a previously unreleased studio song 'A Million Miles', which was credited to the whole band. Why 'A Million Miles' wasn't included on the album over Way's relative clunker 'Too Much Of Nothing' is mystifying. Perhaps it was time or budget constraints; maybe the band wanted to stay clear of accusations of being too ballad orientated. Whatever the reason this song is one of UFO's strongest non-metallic tracks and easily holds its own with 'Out In The Street' or 'I'm A Loser'. If 'Too Much Of Nothing', and the instrumental 'Between The Walls', had been ditched in favour of this gem it would have led to a much stronger second side, as was.

Force It is more focused and heavier overall than *Phenomenon*. It consolidated the band chemistry and concentrated on concise high-quality rock songs. The absence of a cover version allowed more space for the band's own writing talents and showed that Schenker and Mogg were a significant musical force to be reckoned with. A classic band is always more than the sum of its parts and here the seeds of true greatness were sown.

'Let It Roll' (Schenker/Mogg)

A single distorted guitar note bleeds into feedback and the fastest opening track by the band speeds away on a massive rocking groove. Mogg's semi-shouted vocals are in the upper reaches of his range, his lyrics concerned with fast cars, a favourite subject. The low-pitched chorus backing vocals are the only poor feature of this explosive track. There is a blistering, short guitar solo, another impassioned verse, and the song kicks into another riff which has a surprising 'metallic-Celtic' feel to it.

And then, unexpectedly, the instrumental slows into a half-speed ballad tempo with harmonised guitar lines providing a softer texture against the restrained bass, acoustic six-string, and drums. Schenker's gift for melody shines here; the overlaid guitars create an impressive, lush interlude and his solo cuts through the underlying harmonisation with passion and precision.

This is a brief period of calm before another storm, as a pulverising, power-chord progression is unleashed with Schenker playing in unison, and then harmonising with himself. The opening rhythm breaks back in again with a disappointing reprise of the first verse, the 'Celtic riff' brings the song to a tight, effective end, and all of this is achieved in under four minutes. UFO had a knack for killer opening tracks and 'Let It Roll' is the first of what would become a proud tradition.

'Shoot Shoot' (Schenker/Mogg/Way/Parker)

After the light, shade, and relative complexity of the opener, this sprightly major key-based mid-tempo rocker follows a more traditional verse/chorus structure. Its two-chord motif would be used to huge commercial success by Brian May playing variations of it for various Queen hits, ('We Will Rock You', 'Hammer To Fall' and 'It's Late'.)

Vocally 'Shoot Shoot' is in a more comfortable range for Mogg and his refrain is superb, 'Though she's got a pistol, laid it down on me, and she said....shoot, shoot, shoot it for me, you've gotta, shoot it for me'. There is a magnificent grinding guitar riff which moves back into the second verse of this story of romantic betrayal. Midway through the happy raucousness, Schenker produces another jaw-dropping solo leading to the third verse and the song's conclusion, 'Gotta get a fast ride out of here', as it fades away on a return of the grinding riff.

'Shoot Shoot' soon established itself as a concert favourite, usually appearing as an encore. The transition between *Phenomenon* and where the band was headed was never so clear as with these two songs.

'High Flyer' (Schenker/Mogg)

This heartfelt ballad could have featured on *Phenomenon*, being similar in style to several of that album's tracks. It begins with a gently picked baroque style acoustic guitar sequence consisting of three bars in 4/4 time and a single bar of 3/4, which is joined in counterpoint by Way's high register bass line. Changes in time signature would occur elsewhere in the band's repertoire, and show a degree of subtle, skilled musicianship that placed UFO above their contemporaries without coming across as being 'prog-rock-clever'.

Mogg's exceptional vocals and lyrics, 'High flyers, wailing birds, I'm so far out to sea', lead into another wonderfully melodic guitar solo. There is nothing flashy here; Schenker's playing is restrained without being polite, powerful without aggression, and the texture is further expanded by a dated sounding mellotron providing a pseudo-choral backing. Mogg's poetic words, 'Look to summer, go so fast, seems I've never seen you', together with the harmonised chorus, 'And you're every melody, with the sea tides tossing free, never, never holding back, rock 'n' rollers drift by', are stunning. The song fades out on a reprise of the introductory chord sequence and is another example of the band's understated class.

'Love Lost Love' (Schenker/Mogg)

'Love Lost Love' opens with heavy upfront power-chords, a major key, and a fiery guitar melody which destroys the peaceful mood. Mogg conveys the desire to succeed in the music business amidst the many distractions available. The verse is punchy, poppy and insistent, the chorus bright with a sing-along refrain, and the brisk, shrill-toned guitar solo makes its point without wasting a single note.

'Love Lost Love' is a good track which had the potential to be a single with its pop-sheen but it lacks the depth of quality of the songs which have preceded it. The song's ending is a near repeat of the introduction and Schenker adds in a final power chord punch as the rest of the band fades away. It sounds like an overlooked production error.

'Out In The Street' (Way/Mogg)

If proof were needed of Mogg's vocal and lyrical prowess, then you need listen no further than this song. Over a sublime keyboard melody and hypnotic hi-hat rhythm his voice soars, name-checking silent film era stars Buster Keaton and Louise Fazenda in this ode to the long-gone vaudeville years of entertainment; unusual subject matter for a rock song, and something for detractors of heavy rock bands to pay attention to when criticising the genre.

This was the first time a blend of subtle keyboards and blazing guitar were utilised and this would quickly lead to the expansion of the band to a five-piece. The increased dynamic and textural range provided by a keyboard player would enable Schenker's live solos to shine even more as the mid-range frequencies of the backing music would not disappear.

The heavy bridge, 'Out in the streets for just one more matinee...', leads into the guitar solo which is a master class in two acts; the slower first section over the verse chord structure is a diatonic based melody with plenty of musical space in-between the phrases, full of vibrato and expression, whilst he lets fly in the 'double time' chorus section. But it is never 'notes for notes' sake', there is phrasing and accuracy in the melodic flurries cascading from his Gibson Flying V even when the band is in full rock mode.

'Out In the Street' works magnificently as it marries dynamic control to both aggressive and subtle playing, and a superb vocal performance which elevates the song into a class of its own.

'Mother Mary' (Schenker/Mogg/Way/Parker)
Back in the land of all-out metal for what was the opening track of side two is this slab-riffed monster. Mogg spits out the lyrics, with Schenker adding biting fills, and the track moves into a sinewy, chromatic riff as this incendiary song takes hold. This leads into another verse, 'World held up to ransom, a quick hand and a gun', with the secondary riff developed into a longer set of phrases before the dynamics drop down over the short chorus, which again features backing vocals of dubious quality, 'Mother Mary, could you ever really feel the same?'.

Schenker goes full tilt at his solo with short, achingly emotive, harmonised phrases at its close providing further proof that he was a musician of unique talent, potential, and taste. A repeated first verse and chorus appear over the relentless rhythm, with the guitarist on fire yet maintaining control as his harmonised phrases ring out in the coda section and suddenly it's all over.

The range of technique and musicianship both in composition and performance is excellent and raised this song into 'instant classic' status amongst fans. 45 years on, 'Mother Mary' is the opening number on the band's farewell tour and, despite its age, the song sounds neither dated nor tired.

'Too Much Of Nothing' (Way)
Left to his own devices, Way is not a great songwriter. 'Too Much Of Nothing' is the relative dud of the album. It would have sounded better on *Phenomenon* by increasing the hard rock quota of tracks. There's nothing wrong with the song, *per se*, but the below-par lyrics and a reliance on three chords leave it sounding basic when compared to the rest of the album. The band acquit themselves well; Parker's driving drumming with his recently acquired double bass kit adds real power, and Schenker inevitably raises the quality when his solo section begins.

After the initial straightforward melody, the instrumental moves into another mesmerising passage, similar to but distinct from 'Let It Roll'. Controlled feedback is used as a melodic tool over tribal drum rhythms, and Way's bass moves centre stage for a simple, effective solo line. It's a refreshing change and is the best part of the song creating a different mood to the heaviness of the verse and choruses which makes a brief return with the refrain, 'The whole world keeps on turning, I just roll along', to round off the track. 'Too Much of Nothing' is adequate, and instrumentally strong in places, but everything else on *Force It* is just so much better.

'Dance Your Life Away' (Schenker/Mogg)
This is another up-tempo, major key song with a lively funk-based riff over which Mogg spins his tale of the dance marathons of days gone by and the potential dangers of going too far for too long without consequences. With hindsight, this would prove to be prophetic for the singer. There's an underlying pop feel here helped along by Parker's lively use of hi-hat in the verses, even though the tempo feels more leaden in the organ-heavy bridge section.

   The track then moves into a further funky riff played in octave unison by Schenker and Way, before the prominent solo which alternates between the 'creamy' neck pick-up sound, and the sharper tone of the bridge pick-up. This crashes back into the opening riff and a return to the verse/chorus/bridge structure, with the song fading on the octave-unison riff. 'Dance Your Life Away' is a climb back up the quality ladder but only makes it as far as 'Love Lost Love'.

'This Kid's' (Schenker/Mogg) / 'Between The Walls' (Schenker)
UFO's continuing growth and versatility is illustrated here, as the opening has guitar and bass playing the initial complex riff in unison with three bars of 6/8 time and a single bar of 5/8 – which explains why it's difficult to bang your head to it. The song settles into a steady 6/8 groove, and a huge, syncopated ostinato over which Mogg's powerful voice is once again at the top of its game with memorable lyrics, 'Hole in my pocket, hole in my arm, all that's left when life's lost its charm'.

   After the second verse and chorus Schenker solos over an immense boogie rhythm. It's controlled, aggressive, and impressive, and given that the majority of his playing is over a single minor chord rhythm for nearly a minute and a half, it underlines the guitarist's ability to *create* without ever resorting to any blues-based clichés.

   At 3.44, the song's natural end, the music segues into 'Between The Walls', a mellotron and harmonised guitar instrumental with restrained bass and drum accompaniment which seems to have been tacked on without musical purpose. The tempo is on the slow side, the feel being one of comedown from the excitement and energy of what has gone before. The playing is immaculate, but it does drift on for nearly three minutes without going anywhere. At 5.33 the dual lead guitar melody ends, and the backing instruments carry on for another 45 seconds to a slow fade. It's an unusual and puzzling end to what has been a magnificent album of explosively melodic rock songs.

Non Album Track
'A Million Miles' (Schenker/Mogg/Way/Parker)

This discovery is a superb mixture of ballad and rocker which starts quietly, with strummed acoustic guitar and piano providing an American country-style undertone. It builds gradually into a slow speed stunner with Mogg in exceptional vocal and lyrical form, his phrasing of the lines 'But you see you mean everything to me, I want you by my side' being masterful. As the song becomes heavier, the chorus features the beautifully sung lyrics 'If we turn a million miles away, just a shoestring for a name'.

Schenker's solo, whilst clearly still at the 'demo' stage, maintains the country feel and is inevitably strong on melody and vibrato. 'A Million Miles' is another gem which has natural bedfellows with 'Out in The Street' or the forthcoming 'I'm a Loser'

No Heavy Petting

Personnel:
Phil Mogg: vocals
Michael Schenker: guitars
Danny Peyronel: keyboards and vocals
Pete Way: bass
Andy Parker: drums
Recorded at Morgan Studios, London
Produced by Leo Lyons, engineered by Mike Bobak
Released on the Chrysalis label: May 1976
Highest chart places: USA: 169, UK: Did not chart

The third and final vinyl produced by Leo Lyons for UFO is also the strongest; despite only two of its songs featuring on *Strangers, No Heavy Petting* shows yet more growth and maturity for the band. The inclusion of a permanent keyboard player was a major step in arriving at an 'ultimate' sound and eventual line-up. An increase in budget and studio time led to a bolder, brighter and, at times, spectacularly heavy record, with massive riff rockers, two excellent ballads, and a couple of lighter pop-rocking tracks.

The new recruit was Argentinean born Danny Peyronel, formerly of the Heavy Metal Kids. Keyboards had been explored on *Force It* and the consequent broadening of sound provided by additional instrumentation allowed Schenker greater creative scope. Peyronel was also a significant songwriting contributor and, whilst his time with the band was only brief, (September 1975 to July 1976,) the imprint he left behind has been maintained to this day. Ever since *No Heavy Petting* UFO has operated as a quintet or a four-piece with an additional musician playing keyboards.

Hipgnosis was retained for another outing as cover designers, this time coming up with a weird image involving a short-haired brunette lady and a puzzled looking monkey exchanging bodily fluids, possibly blood, via clear plastic tubing. The rear cover had the five band members in a surreal 'rock musicians actually enjoying themselves' moment. Peyronel, Parker, Mogg and Way are experimenting with similar tubing, Schenker is an entertained onlooker.

A remastered CD version of *No Heavy Petting* was issued in 2007 including five previously unreleased songs; two cover versions, ('All or Nothing' and 'Have You Seen Me Lately Joan'), and three original compositions, ('French Kisses', 'Do It If You Can', and 'All The Strings'.)

No Heavy Petting is an overlooked classic. It's an improvement on elements of *Force It*, especially in the production department, and remains an important stepping-stone towards what many regard as the best version of the band. Whilst not possessing as many classic songs in terms of exposure on *Strangers*, it has a remarkable cohesion, and further cements the band's reputation as the ones to watch.

'Natural Thing' (Schenker/Mogg/Way)

First up is this riotous riff-fest of a track. Immediately sounding fresher and heavier, Schenker's double-tracked riff grinds away whilst Way and Parker lay down powerful rhythmic backing, and Mogg weaves his warning ode to the dangers of enjoying too much female company whilst on the road. 'Natural Thing' is a fabulous song, insistent and urgent, cranking up a gear and a key before moving into a sing-a-long chorus. This adds further guitars, finishing up on another great riff with the keyboards becoming more prominent as Mogg's voice drops down to a spoken 'What you're doing'.

Following another verse, bridge and chorus, with the lyrics being neither special nor memorable, the guitar solo is concise and controlled. The chorus returns and the song begins to fade on the final riff section with tasteful slide guitar, and Mogg now singing the 'What you're doing' refrain.

Heavy, melodic and memorable, 'Natural Thing' is just what is needed for an album opener – so much so that it was the first song on the vinyl issue of *Strangers*, although suffering a demotion to fifth position when the remastered CD version appeared.

'I'm A Loser' (Schenker/Mogg)

This is the unofficial cousin of 'Out in The Streets' with its use of dynamics and variance of textures, at times quiet and subtle, then loud and powerful. Beginning with a strummed acoustic guitar, Schenker then adds evocative electric slide lines, Way's bass is prominent and Mogg's vocals lay bare the tale of a teenager, alone and seeking company in London on an icy winter's night. Adding arpeggiated keyboards, the song builds with 'Hard times out on the street, hard times, hard to beat', before moving into the aggressive 'I'm a loser' chorus with Mogg's voice just soaring. There's a return to the quieter verse before another climb into a repeat of the bridge and the chorus.

Schenker's slide guitar begins the solo section. He moves into a series of excellent, fast phrases, always melodic, controlled and in keeping with the song which peaks with the repeated 'Loser, I'm a loser' refrains over his playing. There is some excellent interplay between rapid keyboard flourishes and bruising power-chord stabs leading to a final brilliant solo and a tight ending. 'I'm A Loser' is another superb example of UFO's ability to mix melody, dynamics and great songwriting into a single compelling performance.

'Can You Roll Her' (Peyronel/Mogg/Parker)

A thunderous blast of aggressive keyboards, guitar, bass and drums opens this urgent tale of a motorcycling narrator being pursued by the law. Rapid, heart-pumping drums and the continued use of a guitar slide emphasise the tension of this exciting track. After a brief, furious drum break Schenker's solo is astonishing, wrenching notes from his guitar with ease, his final extended run falling into a repeat of the chorus over a rising slide guitar glissando, and it's all over in less than three minutes. This is the fastest song the band ever recorded and is a mini-masterclass in melodic speed metal before the genre was even invented.

'Belladonna' (Schenker/Mogg)
As if setting out to prove they are masters of contrast UFO completely wrong-foots the listener with this understated ballad. Bereft of drums or percussion, 'Belladonna' has a baroque feel in its consistent use of semi-quaver rhythms in the keyboard and guitar parts. Mogg's lyrics are at a peak here, especially in the chorus, 'Out of reach, out of touch, how you've learned to hate so much', with Peyronel's stylish playing adding much to the atmosphere.

Schenker's slow powerful solo melody is interspersed with his trademark 'seagull cry' phrases as keyboard strings are added to the texture. The guitar joins the keyboard accompaniment in a reprise of the chorus which fades with Way's bass providing a simple, impressive counterpoint. 'Belladonna' is a beautiful, affecting piece of work which shows another side to the band amidst all the surrounding heaviness, 'Exhibit A' being...

'Reasons Love' (Schenker/Mogg)
...absolutely brutal. This is UFO at their most aggressive, the opening riff the aural equivalent of being run over by a tank which is having a bad day. Parker drums with barely contained viciousness and the overall sound is as dry as the Sahara. The verse vocals are double-tracked to great effect, and the refrain has Mogg spitting out the memorable lyrics, 'Causes you indulge in, parents try to get you out of these jams, but you've got that epitaph, They won't understand'.

Schenker's amazing solo is shrill, fast, and ferocious, suddenly changing phrasing and sound to a smoother scale-based pattern with reverb appearing effectively in the mix. Abruptly a new 'heavier-than-Sabbath' riff is played four times and then it's straight back to the verse and the chorus with the song coming to a breathless stop after a single final play through of the 'Sabbath' riff.

'Reasons Love' is a masterpiece of heavy rock composition, powerful vocals, and jaw-dropping solo prowess, and it's a mystery why this never made it higher up the pecking order of live material. It has so much going for it as an out-and-out metal masterpiece that further recognition is well deserved. Had it been included on *Strangers* it would have been no more than it warranted.

'Highway Lady' (Peyronel)
Opening up the former side two and heavy on keyboards and full of exuberance, this major key rocker grooves along with energy and precision. 'Highway Lady' is a joyous romp of a song, with part of the chorus having a half-tempo feel to temporarily slow the urgent pace.

The lyrics, concerning the female companionship which can be obtained on a short-term financial basis, are inconsequential fluff. Mogg had nothing to do with them and it shows, but all is forgiven when Schenker's full-tilt solo comes crashing in, peeling off notes before moving into a fast melodic conclusion.

A slight step down in the overall songwriting quality that dominated 'side one', this track could well be UFO sharpening their collective eye on the potential of the US market. As a rock song, it's another high energy, sub-four-minute feast.

'On With The Action' (Schenker/Mogg/Peyronel)
Another change of mood and style here as a slow riff wrenches open an unsettling tale of inner-city disturbance. Schenker holds back, allowing long sustained phrases to lead into Mogg's vicious vocals which paint various urban scenes, all of them bleak. Unfortunately, the backing vocals in the chorus sound like they were added after a particularly successful pub break, although Mogg's final chorus line, 'It's down our street, is it in yours yet' is especially effective.

'On With The Action' is a magnificent, malevolent beast of a track which refuses to break into anything faster or more spectacular, it just sits there, growling away. Schenker's main solo is one of his slowest and yet most effective to date. Only in its second half does he fill some space with trademark patterns, finishing off with a bewildering blizzard of notes falling into a reprise of the chorus. There's a slow fade to black with no resolution to the urban dystopia, the song acting as a lyrical scene-setter for 'Lights Out'.

'A Fool In Love' (Miller/Fraser)
What is it with this band and cover versions? You've just unleashed six superb rock songs of differing hues, a single beautiful ballad, and then you douse the fire with this damp squib? 'A Fool In Love' is a routine blues-rock number, with unspectacular performances from all involved. Nobody is actually slacking here – it's just that compared to the uniform excellence that has preceded it, who thought that including this track was a good idea? And why? Luckily 'A Fool In Love' is over in under three average minutes but, looking at what else was on offer by way of the bonus self-penned studio tracks, it's bewildering that this number was allowed to make it onto the album instead.

'Martian Landscape' (Peyronel)
This minor epic opens with atmospheric keyboards, while a gently strummed acoustic guitar and subtle bass and drums join as the backdrop to Peyronel's paean to his home country. The lyrics are sparse and evocative, and Mogg sings with a regretful tone, restrained and emotive. The mood moves upwards with 'So let it be a small haven, big in your heart', over a slow off-beat staccato rhythm, and a massive chorus crashes in with Mogg giving full rein to his emotional range.

This is followed by a return to the opening with, sadly, a reprise of the first verse. Some new words could surely have been found here, as it smacks of a lack of inspiration. But this is small criticism as the bridge and the chorus make a welcome return, and Schenker propels the song to its faded ending with a counterpoint harmonised melody, soaring with reverb over Mogg's repeated 'Martian landscape' interjections. It is a fabulous, unexpected and surprisingly uplifting end to this masterful collection.

In 2014 Danny Peyronel (vocals), Laurence Archer (guitar), Rocky Newton (bass) and Clive Edwards (drums) formed X U F O and issued an EP *House of X* which included a reworking of 'Martian Landscape'. The song is transformed into a consistently heavy track which dispenses with the light and shade of the original but brings out all its inherent power and passion. It's well worth hunting out.

Non-Album Tracks
'All Or Nothing' (Marriot/Lane)
UFO's re-interpretation adds little to The Small Faces' 1966 original beyond some crunchy rhythm guitar and a harmonised guitar solo reminiscent of Thin Lizzy.

'Have You Seen Me Lately Joan' (Miller)
This is a turgid, bore-a-thon account of Frankie Miller's more up-tempo original, where Mogg appears to have recorded his vocals after a none-too-brief pub stop, or a very deep sleep. Or both.

'French Kisses' (UFO)
This is a lively, lightweight rocker with a glistening pop sheen. Again, Schenker channels his inner Robertson/Gorham style twin-guitar attack in the solo section. It's no lost classic by any means, but it would have made an interesting addition to the album by adding further musical diversity, and could easily have replaced the unnecessary 'A Fool In Love'.

'Do It If You Can' (UFO)
'Do It If You Can' is apparently another all-band composition which starts with up-tempo bass and drums before moving into a glam-rock style groover. Whilst the lyrical refrain, 'Tonight, tonight, we're gonna make it girl', is clichéd, this is another rock-with-added-pop number which could have served the album well. Schenker doesn't have a solo as such and consequently, the play-out feels incomplete.

'All The Strings' (Peyronel)
This highlights Peyronel's ability as a composer, the song coming close to the feel of some of Elton John's big mid-1970's ballads. If 'All The Strings' had made it onto *No Heavy Petting*, and it should, it would have been a rarity in the UFO canon, being devoid of guitar, as neither acoustic, electric rhythm nor solo feature.

Mogg's vocal images of touring America are evocative, ('Sunset lights still dancing on the runway'), and ('Are you someone, are you something, have I seen your face before?'). Peyronel's piano dominates the mix until the chorus ups the ante, organ is added to the texture and a long play-out hints at where Schenker could have shone.

Lights Out

Personnel:
Phil Mogg: vocals
Michael Schenker: guitars
Paul Raymond: keyboards and guitar
Pete Way: bass
Andy Parker: drums
Recorded at AIR London Studios
Produced by Ron Nevison
Mixed at PYE studios, London
Released on the Chrysalis label: May 1977
Highest chart places: USA: 23, UK: 54

Lights Out is viewed by many fans as UFO's ultimate studio achievement where all their stars of potential, talent, and hard work aligned. Their breakthrough album (especially in the States) contains three undeniable rock classics in 'Too Hot To Handle', 'Love To Love' and the title track, which remain in the setlist to this day. On the vinyl issue *Strangers* scoreboard, *Lights Out* is second with three entries compared to two from *Phenomenon*, five from *Force It*, and only a pair from *No Heavy Petting*. With this album the band went up several gears as a result of significant alterations to what had been their *modus operandi*.

The most important change was one of personnel. The replacement of keyboardist Danny Peyronel with multi-instrumentalist Paul Raymond, who had come to the band's attention via stints with Savoy Brown and Chicken Shack, was a game-changer. He could move between emotive keyboard passages, hard-rocking rhythm guitar parts, and also sing backing vocals. In a live setting, this was the best of all worlds for UFO and enabled a fuller and more representative studio sound to be delivered on stage.

Another significant transformation was the appointment of a new producer in hard taskmaster Ron Nevison who had an impressive track record as an engineer for Bad Company, The Who and Led Zeppelin. There was also a much bigger budget from Chrysalis, a different recording environment, and the addition of orchestral horn and string arrangements (by Alan McMillan) to some of the songs.

Hipgnosis turned in another striking cover. The front featured Mogg and Schenker inside the turbine room at Battersea power station, London. Mogg is in the foreground, face out of shot and overalls unbuttoned to the waist. Schenker is in the distance with his back to the camera, disrobing. Way, Parker, and Raymond do not feature. On the rear, all five appear, fully clothed, in individual portrait-style photos against more interior power station backdrop.

Whilst *Lights Out* is rightly accorded many accolades it isn't the best Schenker period album. When it's good, it's better than anything else they had previously recorded, especially in terms of overall production quality, but it is let down by two pedestrian tracks, and a completely unnecessary cover version. When the band is on fire on the major songs, it brings into sharp focus how ordinary the comparative lightweights are.

Given Schenker's ability to write melodic and involving instrumentals, it would have been a better idea to include one of his heavier compositions. The masterful 'Into The Arena' from his first solo album was just three years away and a similarly anthemic piece, if there were no better songs available, would have been very impressive. 'Getting' Ready' could have been relegated to the second track on 'side two', and 'Alone Again Or' dispensed with altogether.

Lights Out was reissued in a remastered CD format in 2008 with the addition of some previously unreleased live recordings of the title track, 'Getting' Ready', 'Love To Love', and 'Try Me', but without any demoed but rejected studio songs. The album is a consummate piece of work but is *just* beaten to the post by *No Heavy Petting* in terms of consistency of songwriting quality. Luckily even better was to come...

'Too Hot To Handle' (Way/Mogg)

First out of the blocks is the album's most basic and yet insistently satisfying rocker. A stadium-sized crowd-pleaser built around a brilliantly simple riff, 'Too Hot To Handle' hits the ground running and never lets up. Mogg spits out his obscure lyrics, 'Caught in the crossfire, a warning fight, legends make or break game, swept up on the rolling waves of the night, the paper chase for fame', in this ode to the downsides of venereal disease. The sing-a-long chorus is irresistible and is clearly designed for audience participation.

At the start of the second verse, a better sounding drum part suddenly emerges, as someone shifted a fader up in the studio. Mogg provides a sexually provocative bridge section, and Schenker's first solo enters the fray. It is melodic, fast but not excessively so, and totally in keeping with the song. Solo over the instrumental continues with a reprise of the bridge section chord sequence, Parker's percussive power propelling this secondary riff along. Mogg gathers breath for the final verse and repeated chorus, and Schenker adds an interweaving solo to the end.

'Too Hot To Handle' is a fantastic opening track; exciting, powerful, and melodic, it continues the band's fine tradition for hitting the listener between the ears right from the start.

'Just Another Suicide' (Raymond)

If this song was heavier, it would be a more credible proposition. As it stands the juxtaposition of dark lyrical subject matter set against a brisk driving rhythm in a major key is counter-intuitive. 'Just Another Suicide' gives the impression of being inspired by 'Highway Lady' but ends up coming across as a 'diet' version, with stodgy strings attached. A different set of lyrics and a harder guitar sound would have turned it into a worthwhile rocker and, whilst it is melodic and catchy in places, there is just too much going on, instruments compete for sonic space, and dynamic control is largely absent.

Schenker delivers the obligatory solo, albeit in a relatively unspectacular fashion, and this alone manages to lift the song from the prosaic. Following a repeat of the chorus, there is a brief, quieter interlude featuring just piano and strings, but then there's a reprise of the first verse and bridge.

The overall effect is one of 'kitchen sink' inclusion rather than sparklingly sharp instrument placement, with too much emphasis being placed on orchestration and not enough on barely tamed rock energy. As the song enters the final furlong, Mogg's repeated 'Another suicide' refrains are effective, as more instrumentation is added to the texture before the fade. A remix *sans* strings and with more rock guitar would have been intriguing.

'Try Me' (Schenker/Mogg/Raymond)

'Try Me', the album's only true ballad, started life as a guitar instrumental before being handed over to Mogg and Raymond who turned it into an emotional roller-coaster. Opening with some beautifully played piano phrases in slow 4/4 time, Mogg's vocal delivery and lyrics, 'Tell me why, we're never more than strangers, tell me why, you never let it show', over subtle 6/8 arpeggios are first class. Here the string section is sublime and supportive as the chorus shifts into the relative major key after the minor tonality of the verse. It is supremely effective.

Another verse and chorus lead into Schenker's solo, which he has described as his favourite of his work with UFO. Initially understated, involving a few tasteful notes and short phrases, it gradually builds both in tone and intensity. When the drums and bass enter and the track opens up, he lets rip, his playing drenched in emotion as he wrings every ounce of feeling from his guitar, with space between the phrases as he lets the music ebb and flow. This is exactly how an electric guitar solo should be played, a perfect complement to the heartfelt ballad of which it is an integral part.

'Lights Out' (Schenker/Mogg/Parker/Way)

'Lights Out' is the fastest, most urgent song on the album. Mogg's evocative lyrics, inspired by the rise of the right wing National Front, once again on the theme of street violence and civil uprising, are blended with Raymond's distinctive keyboard flourishes. Way and Parker lay down a menacingly memorable rhythmic groove, and there is a supremely catchy crowd-pleasing chorus.

After another driving verse and chorus, Schenker's wah-wah pedal enhanced solo burns all in its path with its repeated fast runs, epic use of vibrato, and whole tone string bends. There's a further chorus, a final verse and chorus, and the song begins to fade as another stunning guitar solo drops phrases around Mogg's haunting 'Lights out, lights out in London' refrains.

'Lights Out' is a giant of a song, devoid of dynamic contrast, manic in delivery, and a fine end to what was the first side of the vinyl album. This is the sound of a band firing on all cylinders with high energy commitment, everyone at the top of their game delivering the goods in a unique and utterly compelling fashion.

Inevitably it would become a concert favourite and remains an enduring, epic slice of the melodic hard rock for which UFO would become justly famous.

'Gettin' Ready' (Schenker/Mogg/Raymond)

'Gettin' Ready' is the album's first major disappointment, a tired trudge of a track which manages to be simultaneously uninspired and uninspiring. The song is a routine 'rock-by-numbers' effort which does its best to be both melodic and memorable but fails to deliver adequately in either department.

Revolving primarily around three chords and an unimaginative lyric it follows a typical verse/chorus/repeat structure. The bridge section is more involving, and the music then drops into a half-tempo instrumental, reminiscent of 'Let It Roll', but nowhere near as good as Schenker throws some sparse phrases against the leaden backing.

There's a return to tedium with another verse, no new lyrics here just retreads of what's gone before, and a final chorus, a few heavy guitar chords, some drum roll fills, and it all comes to a thankful end. 'Gettin' Ready' is one of the band's most ordinary, inconsequential songs and is outshone by everything else on the album. With one notable exception...

'Alone Again Or' (Maclean)

Oh good, a cover version. But it's more than that. UFO set out to record their take on Love's original and end up instead with a virtual sonic photocopy. If you have to record someone else's songs, then at least stamp your own identity on them. It's not as if the band was short on personalities. Here they manage to replicate an unspectacular pop song without imbuing it with any of their own undeniable talents. In the past when they recorded a cover, their own musical muscle would be added to the original, turning it into a definitively UFO version of the song.

Here the only thing of passing interest is how well Schenker can impersonate the trumpet solo and orchestral counterpoint of the original's instrumental section. Ever the perfectionist he does it very well, using controlled wah-wah and meticulous phrasing. But what's the point?

If you need to listen to this song – and you don't – it's on the album *Forever Changes*. If you do decide to send your ears that way, try to figure out how UFO's impersonation is superior. Or even different enough. Aside from a slightly faster tempo, a few power chords here and there, and an irritating tambourine, the two versions are almost identical. In its original format this song was a waste of Chrysalis's vinyl. With the advantages of digital technology it's a button press away from 'Next'.

Fortunately, 'Next' delivers.

'Electric Phase' (Way/Schenker/Mogg)

Just when you thought all hope had packed its bags and left the album for good UFO suddenly remember that they are a hard rock band. Things start to move immediately with another basic Way riff which unleashes the full melodic might of Schenker's slide guitar in this mid-paced growl of a song. Raymond grinds out a suitably dirty funk-style guitar riff as Schenker's air-raid siren impersonations continue, and the song lifts into a magnificent, full-blown, chorus. Mogg is back to sounding like he means it although his theme of telephonic communication is unusual, and some of the lines ('There's no illusion in this world of confusion') are very average indeed.

Schenker's slinky 'cocked' wah-wah solo (where the foot pedal is left in a single tone altering position rather than regularly manipulating the sound,) is stylishly effective, especially with the short harmonised phrases towards the end. This has the effect of lifting the song into the stratosphere as the first verse and chorus are reprised. A veritable orchestra of guitars is overlaid as the song fades, segueing into the opening of a timeless masterpiece...

'Love To Love' (Schenker/Mogg)

Arguably the best epic rock ballad the band could or would ever produce, 'Love To Love' is not only the longest song on any UFO album, (ignoring 'Flying' and 'Star Storm', which is something you should do at all times), it is also their most musically complex and ambitious track.

It begins with a distant harmonised guitar introduction which Schenker had recorded as a demo at home. The unique sound he had captured proved impossible to replicate in the studio, and so the original was used leading into a single gong bang, and some sparse keyboard flourishes before a *Tubular Bells*-style piano ostinato starts to roll. Quiet bass, subdued guitar and subtle drums trick the ears into a false sense of tranquillity.

Then all sonic hell is unleashed as the power-chords barge their way through leading into a huge bulldozer of a riff. An added acoustic guitar melody moves the music through a mixture of 7/4 and 5/4 time signatures. It's clever stuff that doesn't give the impression of showing off, musically it just feels right.

There's a chance to draw breath as the relentlessly heavy groove loosens with a simple, memorable electric guitar melody, with Way's bass moving in counterpoint, as the string section joins the texture leading into Mogg's best vocal and lyrical performance to date. The song moves into 3/4 time for the sublime verse and magical chorus, followed by a beautiful, understated instrumental section before the return to the opening piano refrain and subsequent heavy riffage. The song's second half is almost identical to its first. Mogg excels himself with 'The west bound moon only rises to fall, I lost you and I want you to stay', and the massive chorus, 'Misty green and blue, love to love you', is simply superb.

The closing instrumental section has Schenker finally unleashed as the music builds and builds, his guitar screaming high above the rhythmic backdrop, chords rising and falling like huge ocean waves, before coming to an unexpected and savage halt. Dramatic, spectacular, astonishing, and a fine end to what is, on more occasions than not, an excellent album.

Obsession

Personnel:
Phil Mogg: vocals
Michael Schenker: guitars and flute
Paul Raymond: keyboards and guitar
Pete Way: bass
Andy Parker: drums
Recorded at C.P. McGregors, Western Avenue (Drums), and The West 3rd Carrier
Station, Beverley Hills, Los Angeles, California with the Record Plant mobile
Produced by Ron Nevison
Assistant Engineer: Mike Clink
Mixed at The Record Plant, Los Angeles
Released on the Chrysalis label: June 1978
Highest chart places: USA: 41, UK: 26

Following on from the significant success of *Lights Out*, especially in America,
there was a justifiable feeling within most of the band that their time had
arrived and the rock world was theirs for the taking. And they were right. But
then it was all to change.

The warning signs had been growing for years. The relentless pressure of
touring, writing and recording together since 1973, the growing dependency
on alcohol and drugs as the workload and success levels increased, and the
constantly simmering personality clash between Schenker and Mogg combined
into a perfect storm of tension. Added to this potent mix were Schenker's
problems with stage fright. He was increasingly uncomfortable with his
growing reputation as a 'Guitar God' and left the band just prior to the tour to
promote *Lights Out*.

Paul Chapman, who had joined the band as a short-lived rhythm guitarist
(May 1974 to January 1975), was redrafted at short notice as the lead guitarist
for the tour, much to the consternation of fans. Mindful of how integral
Schenker was to the band's success, and the temporary nature of the tsunami
of popularity they were riding, Pete Way successfully persuaded the German to
rejoin in time for the writing sessions for their next album.

The cover, another perplexing effort by Hipgnosis, introduced the 'lightning
strike' band logo which has decorated all official UFO recordings and
merchandise ever since. The cover photograph, set in an operating theatre,
depicts Mogg and Way, all suited and booted, with greased back hair and ball-
bearings covering their eyes. Schenker stands alone some distance back and
in-between them, a visual metaphor if ever one was needed, looking every
inch the rock star. The ball bearing effect was continued on the back cover
with Raymond and Parker similarly disguised and virtually unrecognisable.

Obsession is the recording pinnacle of the first Schenker era. There are
classic crowd-pleasing anthems, solid groove-based rockers, two excellent
ballads, and a pair of short instrumentals which act as interludes in the

heaviness. There are no cover versions, no 'skip' songs, and the album benefits from a crystal clear hard-rocking production. None of the tracks last over four and a half minutes and there is a greater sense of urgency and energy to the recording than was present on *Lights Out*. The sound is wonderfully 'live' with an added studio sheen, although sometimes overdoing it in the reverb department.

The album's sole contribution to the original *Strangers* track listing was 'Only You Can Rock Me', although a reissued CD version would 'correct' and extend the running order with the inclusion of 'Cherry' and 'Hot 'n' Ready'. The 2008 CD re-issue of *Obsession* does not contain any newly discovered studio tracks but includes previously unreleased live recordings of 'Hot 'n' Ready', 'Pack It Up And Go', and 'Ain't No Baby'.

Overall *Obsession* 'is a more exhilarating, involving experience than its predecessor. Schenker's studio swansong, at least until 1995, featured some of his finest solos, savage riffs, a wonderful sense of creativity, and excellent guitar tones. Mogg's voice has never sounded better, and whilst lyrically he doesn't match the poetic intensity of, say, 'Love To Love', he still proves himself to be one of rock music's most adept songwriters and singers. Way's bass lines are melodic where they need to be and hard-rocking elsewhere. Parker has his best-recorded drum sound so far, and Raymond's contributions show just how essential he had become to the band's sound, style, and songwriting.

'Only You Can Rock Me' (Way/Schenker/Mogg)

Opening with a quasi-Status Quo riff before the rest of the band crash in, 'Only You Can Rock Me' combines hard rock with commercial catchiness, especially in the chorus. Lyrically it's not much to write home about, although Mogg hits a high point in the second verse with his trademark style of singing just off the beat with the lines 'Just like a jewel shines in the night, she burns so hot out under the streetlight'. The melodic refrain of 'We are here and there's no end', where Schenker provides a harmonised melody to Mogg's vocal line, is also irresistible.

After the second chorus, there is an effective breakdown into a keyboard-based instrumental section, Raymond reportedly taking his inspiration from touring comrades Rush. The band dials it down a notch and allows the music to catch its breath before Schenker's astonishing solo storms in, his mesmerising melody being an integral part of the song.

Then there's a reprise of the introduction and a repeat of the first verse. This is an irritating facet of Mogg's writing. On several occasions rather than write a third verse he merely repeats his opening lines as the final verse of a song. Much to the frustration of producers, the vocalist would leave lyrics and sometimes song titles to the very last minute, and at times on *Obsession* it shows. The repeated chorus and refrain leads into a concise ending, the reverb effect on the final sustained 'again', drifting immaculately into...

'Pack It Up And Go' (Way/Schenker/Mogg)

A huge sounding drum introduction and a stupendous funk-based guitar riff open up the album's heaviest track. Lyrically it's either a dig at the first wave of rock superstars (think Stones, Who or Zeppelin), or the casualties of the late 1960s acid scene with some stand-out lyrics, 'You made the impact back in 1969, but now move over, friend I think you've had your time'. Schenker interjects brutal phrases in-between Mogg's fine vocals, notably on the refrains, 'And all our yesterdays, go sailing out of view', and the guitar solo portrays every note as an agony.

It may be a cliché but on *Obsession* Schenker genuinely sounds like a man playing his heart out. It is conjecture, of course, but possibly the ongoing personality clash with Mogg led him to dig deep and deliver the goods on every song on this album. There is too much reverb over this colossus of a track, an accusation which can be levelled against all the heavier numbers. The band were searching for that elusive 'live in the studio' sound, but too much reverberation has the effect of losing some of the clarity of the performances. The ballads would fare better in this regard. There is a slight, ironic hint of Zeppelin in 'Pack It Up And Go', reflected in Parker's relentless rhythms and the spacious sound captured by Nevison, but this in no way detracts from this pulverising track.

'Arbory Hill' (Schenker)

As contrasts go, this is a stark one. 'Arbory Hill' is a short instrumental which combines gently picked acoustic guitar with a flute, both played by Schenker. It's a pleasant, pastoral piece which is as surprising as it is brief, and bears similarities to Alex Lifeson's classical guitar introduction to Rush's *A Farewell To Kings* (1977) where a similar tranquil atmosphere was created. Towards its close, the intonation between the two instruments isn't completely accurate.

'Ain't No Baby' (Mogg/Raymond)

A restrained melodic chord sequence of multiple guitars and counterpointed bass lead into this slow grind of a song. Mogg's bitter vocals are targeted at Chrysalis Records and the level of their promotional activity for another of their signings, The Babys, over UFO. The opening lines 'Hey there now big shot, just listen to me, I know the score and there's no great mystery' has a Pink Floyd-ian level of cynicism to them. Of particular note are the superb backing vocals appearing in the chorus, a feature which is fully realised by Nevison at appropriate junctures throughout the album.

Schenker drops in vicious phrases around the lyrics and, after a return to the subtle introduction, he lets fly with his solo which is neither fast nor showy – it just sits completely within the context of the song. There is a final chorus with an excellent moment at 3.29 where guitar and drums play together in triplets. The song's ending hangs on the last lyrics, 'Stay away forever', with Schenker harmonising the melody line. And as (nearly) always with UFO the music is all about melody, either combined with muscle or treated with relative delicacy. This track, like all of *Obsession*, has a lovingly crafted feel to it.

'Looking Out For Number One' (Mogg/Raymond)

A swathe of lush strings ushers in the album's first ballad. Blending subtle piano, soulful vocals, and tasteful guitar phrases, the song then moves into an uplifting chorus which benefits from the added orchestration. After a second verse and chorus the tempo moves into double time for the bridge section, ('Let's get away right out of here, it's not soon enough for me'), leading into Schenker's short, brutal solo over a heavy descending chord sequence which brings the song into another chorus.

The music shifts to a quiet, beautiful, harmonised guitar duet, before a crescendo into repeats of the chorus which slowly fades. 'Looking Out For Number One' is the longest song on the album and could have been fashioned into 'Love To Love-Two', but the focus of *Obsession* is on concise well-structured songs taking precedence over longer more 'progressive' pieces.

'Hot 'N' Ready' (Schenker/Mogg)

Flipping the vinyl years ago, the fiery opening to this terrific rocker has Schenker playing with passion, fire and flow, before hitting a low-down and dirty riff propelled by Parker at his percussive best. Lyrically, as can be assumed from the Whitesnake-like title, this isn't Mogg in his finest muse. His lyrics sound like they were at the scribbled stage and required more work, but the rest of the song rocks along magnificently.

In the solo section the introduction is reprised before Schenker pulls all manner of fast, melodic, and screaming phrases from his guitar over a solidly rocking rhythm section. There's a repeat of the chorus, a breakdown into the opening riff, and a long fade where several Schenkers trade licks with each other. The fade is so well executed that the song finishes exactly where the next track begins, an excellent example of classy record production.

'Cherry' (Way/Mogg)

'Bass' and 'solo' are not normally two words you want to read in the same sentence, but UFO has the capacity to surprise. Here Way's unusual, hypnotic solo introduction is the atypical, highly effective backbone to this tale of a stripper dancing in a bar. 'Cherry's' power is generated by absence, allowing dynamic contrasts to be maximised to their full effect. There's light, shade, and space in this excellent rocker with power-chords and drums puncturing the atmosphere. A wonderfully melodic refrain leads into the full-blown chorus.

Despite following a conventional verse/chorus structure 'Cherry' feels very different, especially in the bridge section where the music moves up a key, and the entire band sound on fire, 'Come on Cherry, let's make it together, out of the neon and into my life, we can't play this game forever'. This leads into an excellent solo and a return to the solitary bass opening. Disappointingly we have another example of Mogg repeating himself in the final verse rather than concluding the story, the music finishing with a sudden syncopated stab of chords.

'You Don't Fool Me' (Raymond/Parker/Mogg)

There's a deliciously low-slung funk feel to 'You Don't Fool Me', the riff grinds away as vocal and guitar phrases are exchanged over titanic drumming, and a head-nodding, foot-tapping groove. Again the lyrics won't be winning any prizes, although Mogg's perfectly phrased delivery of the lines, 'Just got to have you, you drive me crazy' encapsulates the song's subject matter.

The chorus again benefits from sublime backing vocals although they are well back in the mix. The guitar solo soars as the instrumental shifts through three key changes, before returning to the opening riff, verse and chorus, the rhythm driving along incessantly. Towards the end of the track, the repeated 'You don't fool me' refrain has Schenker creating in spectacular fashion before another abrupt stop.

'Looking Out For Number One' (Reprise) (Schenker/Raymond)

This short piece mixes Schenker's tasteful 'cocked-wah' tone slide playing with Raymond's piano accompaniment, and the well-orchestrated strings in a brief reworking of the ballad's main themes. As with 'Arbory Hill' it's a period of relative calm before the onslaught begins again, segueing smoothly into…

'One More For The Rodeo' (Way/Mogg)

Another riff with a funky rock feel to it, this mid-tempo groover is heavy on the cowbell, with guitars swooping all over the mix. Lyrically Mogg is back on form here with 'I turned around to the janitor, asked him just how long you'd been dead'. His tone and phrasing manage to imbue everything he sings with class, especially in the choruses.

'One More For The Rodeo', whilst in the second division of UFO songs, became part of their live set during the reunion tours of the late 1990s, along with another often overlooked gem, 'Electric Phase'. The long fade has multiple guitars playing off each other to great effect.

'Born To Lose' (Schenker/Mogg/Raymond)

And so to the closer. A beautifully arpeggiated chord sequence, replete with subtle modulation and a harp in the background, introduces this stunning, hard-edged ballad with Mogg's regret-tinged vocals. The rhythm section joins in on the chorus with the strings enhancing rather than suffocating the song. The inclusion of a harpsichord at this point adds an unusual and enticing baroque feel to the track.

After the second chorus, Schenker's solo is the best of any ballad he recorded with UFO. His playing just drips emotion and there is a superb moment, amongst many, at 2.12, where the string section takes over the end of one of his phrases. When the bass and drums join in, he switches sounds from the smooth neck pick-up sound to the shrill scream of the bridge.

The final chorus with Mogg's lines 'I can never be, I will never be the lonely one' is especially effective, the song ending on a sustained guitar chord slowly fading to nothing. 'Born To Lose' is a surprising end to such a rocking collection but it works as a single, emotive bookend to the rest of the album's brutal heaviness.

Strangers In The Night

Personnel:
Phil Mogg: vocals
Michael Schenker: guitar
Paul Raymond: keyboards and guitar
Pete Way: bass
Andy Parker: drums
Recorded live in the United States, October 1978
Produced by Ron Nevison
Released on the Chrysalis label: January 1979
Highest chart places: USA: 42, UK: 7

The 1970s was the decade of the 'double-live' album. Fans wanted more than the typical 40-minute fare of studio recordings, and the chance to experience the sound of a live concert was compelling. Record companies, only too keen for their next dollar, were happy to comply and it was seen as a badge of honour to be 'big enough' to warrant the issue of such an album. With *Strangers* UFO joined this 'Hall Of Fame' which included the likes of Deep Purple, Rush, Status Quo, Queen, Led Zeppelin, and Thin Lizzy.

The original vinyl release featured performances recorded at The Amphitheatre, Chicago, and The Gardens, Louisville, on the autumn 1978 tour to promote *Obsession*. A subsequent 'expanded' CD release added 'Hot 'n' Ready' and 'Cherry' taken from the same tour.

The brightly coloured iconic album cover, again by Hipgnosis, is an amalgam of many small multi-coloured balls which form images of close-up audience reaction. In the inner sleeve the band is depicted in a similar black and white format left to right it's: Way, Mogg, Raymond, Schenker, and Parker. Overlaying this imagery are plenty of small photographs of the individual members getting on with the action live, as it were.

Despite having recorded a number of concerts, Nevison did not feel he had enough material with which he was happy to issue a full-length double album. In November 1978 the band were ordered back to the studio and new versions of 'Mother Mary' and 'This Kid's' were recorded, with crowd noise being added to fool the listener. And fooled we were. Such a good job was done, that no one was any the wiser until the information emerged in the accompanying booklet to the 2008 re-mastered CD series. Did we feel cheated? Yes, of course, and whilst accepting that there may have to be minor studio enhancements to any live album to put the band in the best (sonic) light, two entire songs is moving the dial way too far.

The pressures which had rebuilt during the recording of *Obsession* spilt over again in the studio mixing sessions for *Strangers*. Schenker was unhappy with some of Nevison's production decisions which, according to differing accounts, varied between the quality of his guitar sound, and being allowed, or not, to 'touch up' some of his work. The ensuing arguments eventually led to him leaving the band again, this time 'permanently'.

In the inner gatefold sleeve confusion was caused with the inclusion of the words; 'Special thanks to our friend and guitarist – Paul Chapman' leading some to speculate that it was Chapman rather than Schenker playing on *Strangers*. The guitar tone is, of course, pure Schenker and the purpose of the credit was to inform fans that Chapman would be the band's permanent guitarist by the time *Strangers* was released, and that a new era was about to begin.

Two singles were released from the album. 'Doctor Doctor', with a live version of 'On With The Action' and the studio version of 'Try Me', reached number 35 in the UK charts whilst 'Shoot Shoot', combined with 'Only You Can Rock Me' and 'I'm A Loser', got as far as number 48.

Strangers regularly features near the top of any 'Greatest Live Album Of All Time' poll, and rightly so. It's fair to say that it is *'almost'* the best live album ever, and if 'Mother Mary' and 'This Kid's' had actually been 'live' or replaced with other songs which were the genuine article, then the *'almost'* could be dispensed with. As it stands *Strangers* is Schenker's swansong as well as being both a fine 'Live Best Of' and a compelling insight into just how good the band was at this, the first of their three peaks.

The overall effect of listening to the live versions of familiar songs is just how much more powerful the band were on stage than in the studio. This improvement is particularly apparent with the songs from *Phenomenon*, and *Force It*; their live counterparts are just explosive, much more vital and aggressive. And they weren't bad to begin with! *Strangers* was reissued on CD in 1999 as an 'expanded' edition which re-sequenced the songs to give a more 'authentic' version of the tour. Of course, if authenticity were the genuine intention then 'Mother Mary' and 'This Kid's' would have been omitted. However, the illusion had to be maintained, at least for the best part of two decades…

In the main, the live versions are structurally identical to the studio originals, with only 'Doctor Doctor', 'This Kid's', and especially 'Rock Bottom' expanding their original format. Comments on individual songs are therefore limited to minor differences, the odd mistake or improvement, and deviations from their studio counterparts.

'Hot 'N' Ready' (Schenker/Mogg)

Given that the sleeve notes to the 'expanded' CD state that this song was recorded on 15 October 1978 in Youngstown, Ohio, it's amusing to hear the familiar announcement that starts proceedings 'Hello Chicago…'

This live version omits the original's high octane instrumental introduction, going straight to the main riff, with Mogg's voice sounding strained as he sings in his higher register. Schenker's solo deviates slightly from the original, especially in the play-out section, the song ending on a single punchy power-chord.

'Cherry' (Way/Mogg)
Recorded in Cleveland on 16 October 1978, Way's bass introduction has some muted backing guitar added and Parker makes a rare error as he misses the second pick-up into the 'We-I go again' section at 3.20. Schenker's solo is close but not identical to the studio version.

'Let It Roll' (Schenker/Mogg)
Mogg tells the crowd that 'This one's off our 'Corset' album' which is followed by a brief respite where microphones need to be changed. The singer is asked by the stage crew to fill in. He responds 'I dunno whether I should tell a few jokes, possibly reveal myself' and then we're off with another thunderous rhythm, a blazing solo, and the 'oasis' instrumental section which has Schenker and Raymond harmonising the original guitar melodies to great effect.

'Love To Love' (Schenker/Mogg)
Mogg introduces 'Love To Love', the epic nature of which is eminently suited to live performance; so much so it has remained in the band's setlist to the present day. Schenker's guitar sound hangs on the edge of controlled feedback in parts of the opening section, and Raymond's fluid keyboard skills are again a vital asset to the overall sound.

This rendition has more of a country feel in the verses than the original, and Schenker's concluding solo soars and screams with even greater intensity. Extending the studio version by an extra ten bars, nothing he plays sounds clichéd. He just digs deeper and deeper into his creative well and the song comes to a quick, savage stop rather than take the clichéd 'big rock ending' route.

'Natural Thing' (Schenker/Mogg/Way)
The original vinyl album opened with the now-iconic call to arms, 'Hello Chicago, will you please welcome from England ... U F O'. However, the 'expanded CD' now has a possibly inebriated Mogg making the amusing announcement 'We've just taken a vote; apparently this is something called "Natural Thing"'. Raymond makes a significant contribution to the overall sound with his backing vocals fleshing out the song, and his ability to switch quickly between guitar and keyboards effectively making him two musicians in one.

In any live setting, a band has to come up with an alternative ending for those studio songs which faded on record, and here Parker adds some characteristic drum fills around repeated power-chords which drive the song effortlessly into.....

'Out In The Street' (Mogg/Way)
This is virtually identical to the original, but the overall delivery is more muscular than the studio version, and the dynamic contrasts between verses and choruses more extreme. Raymond plays some gracefully atmospheric

piano work which blends with the haunting mellotron string sounds over which Mogg's evocative vocals soar in the verses. It's this calculated balance between restraint and power that makes UFO at their best unmatchable.

'Only You Can Rock Me' (Schenker/Mogg/Way)

There is no attempt by Mogg to sell either this song or the new album to the audience by way of an introduction. Instead, Schenker powers in with the opening riff and the band just go for it in joyous style. In the chorus section, it sounds as if, rather than have Raymond take the 'echo' vocal of 'We ... can't wait from day to day', Mogg is singing over himself which suggests either more studio trickery or the possession of a set of vocal cords which defy the laws of biology.

'Mother Mary' (Schenker/Mogg/Way/Parker)

The first of the 'live-in-the-studio' tracks is as powerful as every other song on *Strangers*, but the effect is diluted by the knowledge that this is 'faked', and also that 'Mother Mary' was not on the setlist for the tour. That said it is an immense version and shows the effect Nevison had on sculpting a bigger and better band sound.

What would *Force It* have sounded like with Nevison behind the desk rather than Leo Lyons? Give this and 'This Kid's' repeated listens, filter out the crowd noise, and you will have a fair idea of how huge the early Schenker period albums could have been. To be filed under *if only....*

'This Kid's' (Schenker/Mogg)

The other 'studio live' take is again faster and punchier than the original. Schenker's solo is extended, lasting from 2.23 to 4.11 and his playing is just superb. Listen out for Raymond switching from keyboard to rhythm guitar as the solo commences leading to a beefing up of the sound.

Fortunately, there is no 'Between the Walls' tacked on at the end. *Strangers* contains neither ballads nor instrumentals; these were only ever a feature of the studio albums. Whilst 'Love To Love', 'I'm A Loser' and 'Out In The Street' have their quieter moments, this is in all other respects a full-on hard rock album and is a (mostly) accurate reflection of the live experience for the audience.

'Doctor Doctor' (Schenker/Mogg)

The crowd quickly responds to Raymond's keyboard arpeggios and Schenker's new, and soon to become definitive, opening melody for UFO's most famous song. Raymond's backing vocals are prominent in the 'Doctor Doctor' refrain, and the song's new live ending is distinctive and un-clichéd.

'I'm A Loser' (Schenker/Mogg)

Slurring to the crowd Mogg can't remember which album this song comes from! Schenker's slide guitar joins with Raymond's soft-sounding keyboards.

Unlike the original, there's no acoustic guitar accompaniment to the verses, and no backing vocals in the 'hard times' or 'loser' sections. Schenker inevitably soars in the instrumental sections of the song, and all of *Strangers* is a tribute to the German's creative virtuosity at this stage of his career.

'Lights Out' (Schenker/Mogg/Parker/Way)
The band launches into a thunderous version, which is taken at a faster tempo and with even greater energy than the studio version. When Mogg sings 'Lights out in Chicago' after Schenker's first fast and furious solo, the crowd erupts. This lyric switch would become a staple of future shows where Mogg would substitute whichever location the band were in that night for the original 'London', and get a similar response. Apparently this moment went less well whenever they played in Aberystwyth.

'Lights Out' is UFO at the top of their game, all guns blazing, a totally committed performance with crystal clear vocals, and a pulverising rhythm section enhancing the sonic bombardment. A tight ending rounds off this excellent rendition of a genuine rock classic.

'Rock Bottom' (Schenker/Mogg)
Mogg's calls out to the crowd 'What'd'y'say?' and their response leads into 'You got it, this is something called 'Rock Bottom''. There then follows the definitive live version of this song complete with a new introduction.

Commencing with Parker's driving cymbals, Schenker unleashes a monster of a riff. Whilst not part of the studio recording this addition feels entirely natural and grows organically into the all-conquering master riff with the dual guitar attack of Schenker and Raymond making it doubly effective. The half-tempo bridge section has Raymond returning to his keyboard, with both him and Schenker throwing in phrases around Mogg's classy vocals.

The extended solo starts at 4.07. Schenker allows notes to spread out as he takes his time, building slow melodic phrases and allowing space to also be musical. He gradually builds the intensity as well as switching pick-ups to a smoother sound, his diatonic runs dancing all over the fretboard as Raymond provides a syncopated single chord backing over Way's relentless bass, and Parker's powerful drumming.

At 6.21 there is a more reflective section as guitar and keyboards harmonise melodies, and then tension builds again to a crescendo, and Schenker lets loose, notes scattering and skating everywhere in a firework display of his soloing prowess. The band gathers forces at 8.05 and leads into the next section where further duelling between guitar and keyboard occurs, leading to a spectacular conclusion at 9.02.

The chorus riff is repeated four times, a perfect opportunity for audience participation, the verse riff returns, as does Mogg who delivers a fine reprise of the first verse. The song concludes with a final chorus and a big, controlled ending before a clichéd power-chord and one of those 'as many notes as you've got' climatic guitar endings, as Way's bass ascends, and Parker hits everything he's got hard, followed by a final massive power-chord to finish.

This live version makes the then five-year-old original sound like a well-produced demo, and it was this new version which would stay in the band's set over the ensuing decades. Future guitarists all brought their own individual style and interpretations to 'Rock Bottom' with varying degrees of success, but none would ever better this.

'Too Hot To Handle' (Way/Mogg)

Mogg's introduction, inviting the audience to take a speaker home to save the PA company some work, leads into a fantastically crunchy rerun of this crowd pleaser. This version does not include Schenker's lead phrases in the final chorus, and he plays a different final solo to the original, again switching between neck and bridge pick-ups to produce brighter tones.

'Shoot Shoot' (Schenker/Mogg./Parker/Way)

This is even punchier than the original, faster and more direct. Raymond joins in on the backing vocals, and there is a new ending which features the band holding on a non-tonic chord over which Schenker produces a final virtuosic fretboard display, with two rapid power chords to finish.

Deluxe Edition

In the summer of 2020, news emerged that the concerts which formed most of 'Strangers...' were to be released in their entirety, and in November it finally came to pass. For the serious fan, this is the Holy Grail of Schenker-era UFO. This deluxe release comprises eight CDs with all six gigs, a remastered version of the original album, and an insert booklet with an essay by Michael Hann, which is a familiar retelling of the band's history with some new contributions from Schenker, Mogg, and Parker.

This is a missed opportunity. What would have been a *much* more interesting read would have been Ron Nevison's take on his work with the band. Why didn't the three opening songs taken from 'Obsession' make the cut? Why ignore 'Ain't No Baby' and 'On With The Action' in favour of the faked songs from 'Force It'? What would he do differently with the benefit of hindsight?

Discs one and two are the original 'Strangers...' in a replication of the original gatefold sleeve. It does not need to be spread over two CDs, and the other shows all manage to fit on a single disc. The newly remastered original album sounds magnificent, but it retains the 'studio live' takes of 'Mother Mary' and 'This Kid's' in the running order. Why perpetuate the deception? Yes, 'Strangers...' has been revered for decades now but, for me, it would have been preferable for the crowd noise to have been removed, and the songs placed at the end of the album as 'bonus studio' tracks. There was a chance to set the record straight, as it were, and it wasn't taken. As the new discs bear witness, there was no shortage of other material which could have been put in place of the fakes. Nevison had a rich source of quality performances; all he did was to add production polish to these diamonds.

The 'new' concerts are the real deal. All open with the triple *'Obsession'* punch of 'Hot' n' Ready', 'Pack It Up (And Go)', and 'Cherry', followed by 'Love To Love' and 'Let It Roll'. The middle of the set-lists vary slightly from night to night, and, in the final straight, the audiences are left punch-drunk with the quadruple assault of 'Lights Out', Rock Bottom', 'Too Hot To Handle', and 'Shoot Shoot'.

Disc Three: The International Amphitheatre, Chicago, Illinois

Mogg throws in an amusing lyric change in 'Pack It Up (And Go)'; 'Move over Eric, I think you've had your time'. Hopefully, Mr Clapton was duly offended. The now epic sounding 'Ain't No Baby', dedicated to a 'fellow artist, and Ron Nevison', is a mighty blend of melody and funky heaviness. The chorus to 'Lights Out', where Mogg substitutes 'Chicago' for 'London', is not greeted with the familiar crowd roar. This would have been a Nevison decision back in the studio.

Disc Four: The Kenosha Ice Arena, Wisconsin

This recording has some microphonic feedback issues early on, and, again, 'Ain't No Baby' is a welcome heavy groover. Possibly the decision to omit the opening songs was to prevent *'Strangers...'* from being too *'Obsession'*- heavy. But the album is their finest work, so why not play to your strengths? This show has an identical set-list to the previous night in Chicago, except 'Shoot Shoot', which is not played.

Disc Five: Tomorrow Club, Youngstown, Ohio

This is the first recording to include 'On With The Action'. The malevolent, bluesy feel of the original receives the full live treatment with Raymond moving between guitar and keyboards to great effect. Schenker's solo is a high point amongst the relentless, intense groove; the final keyboard arpeggio segues gracefully into the introduction for 'Doctor Doctor'.

Disc Six: The Agora Theatre, Cleveland, Ohio

Most of this concert had already been released as part of the *Official Bootleg Box Set: 1975-1982*. Here we get the entire gig including 'Too Hot To Handle' and 'Shoot Shoot', which were previously omitted. Along with the Kentucky show, this is the longest disc with fifteen songs, and includes another muscular rendition of 'On With The Action'. The first appearance of 'I'm A Loser' takes the sonic thunder down, at least temporarily. When the chorus kicks in, the song, like all the Lyons-era tracks, is transformed, with Raymond's contribution again proving invaluable. Schenker's live solo is even more astonishingly creative than its studio counterpart.

Disc Seven: The Agora Ballroom, Columbus, Ohio

Another show to include the sublime 'I'm A Loser', also features an alcohol-enhanced Mogg providing plenty of amusing in-between song banter. 'On With The Action' is included in all its brooding magnificence, the keyboard coda again segueing into 'Doctor Doctor'. Schenker's 'Rock Bottom' solo is an outstanding combination of creative melodic flair and near-perfect technique.

Disc Eight: The Louisville Gardens, Kentucky

Described by Mogg as 'one of those numbers written with Ron Nevison in mind', 'On With The Action' is again brutal. Schenker's phrasing and tone are exemplary, both here and across the entire show. 'I'm A Loser' is another gem, the band's control of dynamics and Mogg's emotive voice raising the track to a new level of excellence.

This release shows UFO at their un-(doctor) doctored best, and underlines just how stunning they were on stage at this time. Schenker shines across all the recordings. Never less than masterful, on occasion, his playing is utterly, jaw-droppingly brilliant. But it's not just the 'Schenker Show', the rest of the band are on fire throughout. Mogg is the charismatic frontman and stylish singer. Way propels the lower end along magnificently, no doubt putting as much, if not more, energy into his showmanship as his actual playing. Raymond's contributions on keyboards, guitar, and the occasional backing vocal really fill the band sound out, and Parker is a non-stop energy machine, hitting everything hard, and being the ultimate back-seat driver. This box-set validates the long-held claim that '*Strangers...*' is indeed the greatest live album of all time.

No Place To Run

Personnel:
Phil Mogg: vocals
Paul Chapman: guitar
Paul Raymond: keyboards, guitars and vocals
Pete Way: bass
Andy Parker: drums
Recorded at AIR Studios Montserrat and AIR Studios London
Produced by George Martin for AIR Studios Ltd
Engineered by Geoff Emerick
Released on the Chrysalis label: January 1980
Highest chart places: USA: 51, UK: 11

Following the release of *Strangers,* UFO was one of the rock world's hottest properties, but now they were without the guitarist who had played such a pivotal role in their ascension. Schenker was a perfectionist loner who spoke no English when he joined the band in 1973. He had always struggled with the language barrier, the others' sense of humour, and their close-knit North London ties. When it became clear his decision was final, the band decided to replace him with another foreigner – okay, a Welshman – Paul Chapman.

Having served time with UFO twice already, the former Lone Star guitarist was offered the position on a permanent basis in November 1978. Chapman, as well as being a fine guitarist, was a known quantity for UFO, and he fitted in instantly, his tolerance for alcohol and other substances earned him the sobriquet 'Tonka' after the 'indestructible' toy trucks. In effect, Chapman was already 'one of the boys'.

Further change was in the air. Chrysalis decided that a new producer might elicit the hit single the label craved, and the services of George Martin were obtained. Despite having enjoyed some degree of success with a four-piece Liverpool based guitar band in the 1960s, Martin was a stranger to the world of heavy rock, and it would show. The main recording location was to be Martin's purpose-built studio in Montserrat in the Caribbean, which suited UFO down to the sand.

Hipgnosis was retained for the album's visuals. Their cover, involving a weak play on the album title, showed the band standing outside a disused petrol station at night, whilst the rear sleeve had an alternative view taken from a different angle. Issued in six different colours, the sleeve is the most disappointing of the various images the designers produced for the band. Of course, it was important to show fans the look of the new line-up, just in case anybody was ignorant of Schenker's departure, but as an iconic image for this new incarnation, it's really not their best work.

From the fans' perspective, the weight of expectation was immense. Would Chapman deliver? Yes. Would the band still be as good? Just about, yes. Would Martin's presence deliver the hit single Chrysalis desired? Not really. Without

Schenker or Nevison would UFO be able to come up with a classic to match *Lights Out, Obsession* or *Strangers*? Erm, no.

Chapman hadn't fully spread his writing wings yet, and the majority of the songs are credited to Way and Mogg, with a single, lacklustre entry from Raymond. This is not to denigrate *No Place To Run,* which is a very good, melodic, hard rock album with dynamic contrasts and differing song styles. There are two outright classics, as strong as anything the band had produced before, mixed with mid-tempo rock-with-added-pop-sheen grooves, a couple of gorgeous ballads, an outstanding cover version (I know...!) and a couple of duds. When *No Place To Run* is good, it's very good, but it's just not consistently engaging. It would be a year before the full potential of the 'Chapman era' would be properly unleashed.

Chapman has a very different style and sound to Schenker, but this is not to put them in any sort of pecking order. He is, in his own way, just as good as his predecessor. Martin's production is clever and classy with some inventive touches, but he doesn't bring the band up to the anticipated levels of energy and excitement.

No Place To Run was reissued as a remastered CD in 2009. Along with live recordings of 'Lettin' Go', 'Mystery Train', and 'No Place To Run' there is an alternative studio version of 'Gone In The Night'. The differences between this and the original are minimal, the most notable being the subtle effects added to Chapman's guitar sound.

'Alpha Centauri' (Chapman)
'Alpha Centauri' is the first time a purely instrumental piece of music had opened an album since *UFO1*. It is also the last time an instrumental would feature on a UFO album until 2002's *Sharks*.

Menacingly atmospheric, this short, slow track served as the introductory music for the subsequent tour. Chapman's sustained guitar moves gradually between low single notes over a heartbeat effect which increases tension and, in a live setting, anticipation. It sounds like a muted bass drum but is, apparently, a stool being hit with a dishcloth treated with added studio trickery. Raymond's ethereal keyboards provide a celestial touch, and the music ends with a single low power chord which bleeds into feedback, growing into...

'Lettin' Go' (Way/Mogg)
...a massive grooving riff which reaches a held chord as Chapman pick-scrapes down a guitar string. Mogg's vocals, 'I'm letting go now, don't think I can last, I'm lettin' go now, I've been living too fast', describe the frustrations of day-to-day working life for people for whom money *is* an object. The song rises into a memorable chorus and the scene is set for a classy, driving rocker which powers along with more resonant lyrics, 'I'm working every day, you'd think I was in love'. The second chorus adds a guitar melody over the vocals which

leads into a disappointing repeat of the first verse until Chapman's first proper solo.

Fans unfamiliar with his work with Lone Star may have wondered if he could pull it off. He does, of course, but it is clearly not what Schenker would have produced. Chapman uses a thinner, more compressed tone with equal speed and fluency. He employs a different style of phrasing, utilising massive string bends together with unusual intervals to augment his solos.

'Lettin' Go' ends with some soft-toned guitar arpeggios. It didn't need to, but again its testament to the quality of UFO's arrangements that this short, subtle coda rounds off the opening two tracks effectively without resorting to the clichéd big power-chord ending. Of course on stage, the big power-chord blast was what was needed and delivered.

'Mystery Train' (Parker/Philips)
Okay, this is the exception that proves my 'rule'. In the past UFO's cover versions have disappointed, here it's the exact opposite. Originally recorded by Junior Parker (no relation), and then Elvis Presley, UFO's interpretation is the business and the song would become a stage favourite for the next three years.

Starting with an impressive solo acoustic guitar workout (yes, the boyo can *really* play), Chapman then sits on a gorgeous rhythmic groove over which Mogg's rich, toned voice just soars. There's a brief acoustic flourish, and then 'Train, train' brings in the heavily rocked-up version of the number which moves between a medium tempo in the vocal sections, and half speed for the lead fills. The solo section is full of energy and aggression as Chapman wrings out more rapid phrases. Whilst 'Mystery Train' is a blues 'standard', UFO transform it into a definitively superior version adding a hard rock sheen that just glistens with power.

As the song enters its final phase Mogg repeatedly invokes 'Never again', and Chapman's closing solo features overlaid harmony guitar lines which bring to mind 'Electric Phase'. It's almost certainly a coincidence as at no point does he seek to emulate Schenker in either style or sound. Chapman is clearly his own man, determined to stamp his own identity on the band which he does to great effect.

'This Fire Burns Tonight' (Chapman/Mogg)
Opening with a crowd-pleasing clap-a-long drum rhythm and a melodic guitar sequence which evokes open roads and big American skies, this foot-tapping groover has Mogg describing (some of) the life of a touring band. Probably autobiographical, it's not the wordsmith's finest work, although the lines, 'It's cold, out in the neon, singing blues every night', show once again just how good a vocalist he is. But it's all a bit 'The Boys Are Back In Town' with lyrics like 'Now me and my partners are movin', we run on from town to town', the chorus sounds like it was written for crowd participation, and overall this song is a step-down in quality from what's gone before.

The track is lifted by its instrumental section. Chapman moves into a new chord progression, and Raymond's organ provides an overlaid melody which moves into a powerful guitar solo. In the song's coda, another Chapman solo appears after the repeated lines 'This fire burns tonight, the streets are alight, out of this town we are bursting', and this fades with multiple guitars interweaving in the background. 'This Fire Burns Tonight' comes across as a calculated move towards stadium-sized audience involvement and could have been a much better song with a different lyric.

'Gone In The Night' (Way/Mogg)

A single overdriven guitar progression is joined by keyboards, bass and drums and the song seems to be veering into early-Sabbath territory, the descending chords being reminiscent of Birmingham's finest. But then there is a sudden and surprising 180-degree *volte-face* as the music moves continents and ends up in a Mid-West American bar. Country piano and subtle guitar fills back another of Mogg's relationship lyrics, and the music builds in power as it approaches the chorus, which is played out over the introductory chord sequence. The song moves back into light Americana for a second verse before growing again into another chorus with increased instrumentation.

Chapman's play-out solo is agonised but too brief and continues a pattern, established with 'Lettin' Go', of leaving the centrepiece solo until the final section of the song, a trick which would also feature in 'Young Blood' and 'Anyday'. 'Gone In The Night' joins the collection of hidden UFO gems never performed live, or being historically significant enough to feature on a 'Best Of' compilation, which is a shame as it's a wonderful track with real depth and feeling.

'Young Blood' (Way/Mogg)

Opening what was 'side two' is the song which would have had 'single' scrawled all over the master tape boxes. 'Young Blood' was duly selected, and landed in the UK charts at number 35, leading to an amusingly mimed appearance on *Top Of The Pops* which was, at the time, one of only two television programmes dedicated to popular music, the other being *The Old Grey Whistle Test* on which the new line-up also appeared.

A chugging guitar, bass and drum introduction lends an air of Bon Scott-era AC/DC to the track. Raymond adds backing vocals to the 'Young blood' refrains, and the power builds under the lines 'Another night and I'm thinking what's going wrong, you say you love me but does love take this long?' Musically its standard pop-rock fare, but Mogg's delivery of lyrics like 'I hear the whispers, the candid talking, and I don't know what to believe' rescue it from mediocrity.

Harmony guitar lines are added to the chorus, and piano to the third verse, but despite its melodies and arrangement 'Young Blood' was never likely to become the breakthrough Top Ten hit that Chrysalis desired. It's just not *that* good a song. After the final choruses, the music steps up a key and a gear as Chapman solos. This, again, is too short, the song fading quickly away.

No Place To Run (Way/Mogg)
Along with 'Lettin' Go' the album's title track is other stand out heavy rocker. Beginning with a persuasive chord sequence and lead guitar theme, the scene is quickly established with a menacing groove (a slowed down variant of the Lights Out' rhythm) over which Mogg weaves his tale of gang retribution in a city by night.

Malevolent and unsettling, there is a section of pure brilliance 42 seconds in, 'The other side of midnight, caught in the combat zone, meaning no resistance, you don't stand alone'. Unusually this brief lift is not used elsewhere in the song. Springsteen-Esque in scope and flavour, Mogg's lyrics are sometimes clichéd, 'heart beating like a drum', (do hearts ever beat like anything else in rock songs?), but the repeated 'Jungleland's at the end of the chorus are highly effective.

Following the third verse, there is a swirling, angry Chapman solo followed unexpectedly by a fabulous funky acoustic guitar riff. Again, this idea is not repeated and just sits mid-song as a further indication of melodic class. Given the surfeit of ideas in this number alone, it's a shame that they weren't fashioned into new songs.

The story begins its fateful conclusion, 'Joey's got his name painted on the walls, on the side of buses, subways and tenement halls'. Interestingly the fifth verse of Simon and Garfunkel's 'The Sound of Silence' has the words of the prophets being 'written on the subway walls and tenement halls'. It must be a coincidence – it's difficult to imagine Mogg channelling his inner folk singer here. Similarly, touring partners Rush were referencing this same lyric in their song 'The Spirit of Radio' (*Permanent Waves*, 1980).

After the final chorus, the song fades with repeated 'Jungleland' as Chapman provides a defiant, screaming solo. 'No Place To Run' can be seen as an excellent scene-setter for what would be the following year's masterpiece, 'Long Gone'.

'Take It Or Leave It' (Raymond)
In two words? Leave it. This drippy, country-style ballad disappoints on every level. Raymond's disenchantment with Schenker's departure may well have influenced the quality of his writing, and after this album, he too left UFO to join the Michael Schenker Group in time for their second album, *MSG*.

Lyrically this is desperately flaccid stuff. It centres on the well-worn themes of a man on the road, and the strains on his relationship with a partner back home. Mogg manages to put sufficient emotion into his delivery, and the chorus is heavier with a piano well to the foreground. Then it's back to another couple of desperate verses, a repeat of the chorus, and the song ends as it began, with a whimper. Devoid of a guitar solo, it is the shortest track on the album, but that isn't a good enough reason not to press 'skip'.

UFO ... On Track

'Money Money' (Way/Mogg)

A major key repetitive chord based riff drives this brisk poppy rocker along with the bass prominent in the mix. There are again shades of the 'Lights Out' rhythm underpinning Mogg's bitter lyrics, and the band's sound is treated with subtle modulation effects. Minor interest is maintained during Chapman's solo, and the instrumental section moves up a key with some Thin Lizzy-style harmony guitars leading back into another round of vocals, with a syncopated, sharp ending. It's an adequate song, no more, no less, but UFO is capable of so much more than adequate, as the final track demonstrates.

'Anyday' (Way/Mogg)

After two disappointments the album's third best track, and best ballad, is saved for last. Unusually the verse sections feature just bass and vocals, Mogg's reflecting on the disintegration of a relationship, 'Seem to be so alone, how it feels is nothing new, We're only goin' through the motions, me and you', as he moves into falsetto at the end of each verse. The haunting bass line was played via a Lesley speaker which provides the distinctive, haunting modulation effect.

The rest of the band join in on a magnificent, heavy chorus which ends with a brief twisting guitar solo before fading into a second verse. The chorus returns and repeats with an upwards key change, and Chapman viciously plays the song into the fade. 'Anyday' is another over-looked jewel in UFO's back catalogue and manages to salvage what was the 'second side' of the album which has been more filler than fulfilling.

The Wild The Willing And The Innocent

Personnel:
Phil Mogg: vocals
Paul Chapman: guitar
Neil Carter: keyboards, guitars, and saxophone
Pete Way: bass
Andy Parker: drums
John Sloman: keyboards (uncredited)
Strings arranged and conducted by Paul Buckmaster.
Recorded at AIR Studios London and at Wessex, Utopia, Maison Rouge and Red
Barn Studios
Produced by UFO
Engineered by Steve Churchyard
Released on the Chrysalis label: January 1981
Highest chart places: USA: 77, UK: 19

The stars align again for UFO as they (self) produce the finest of the four
Chapman era albums. *The Wild...* boasts the best studio sound of any of the
band's albums to date, and the songs span the heavy rock genre ranging from
classic melodic riff rockers, progressive style epic, blues grooves, pop-rock
sing-a-long, and an excellent ballad. There is also the occasional doff of the cap
towards New Jersey's finest son.

Criticism has been levelled at the significant Springsteen influence, prefaced
in *No Place To Run,* on Mogg's writing during this period. On one hand, the
singer did grow up in an area of London not known for its largesse, so he may
be interpreting characters and scenes he had to some extent experienced. On
the other, considerably larger, hand are the facts that Springsteen had released
an album called *The Wild, The Innocent, And The E Street Shuffle*, and the
'Jungleland' refrains from 'No Place To Run' is the title of a song on his 1975
album *Born To Run*. You pays your money...

The departure of Paul Raymond led to a permanent replacement eventually
being found in multi-instrumentalist Neil Carter. In addition to playing guitar,
keyboards, and providing backing vocals, he was also adept on both saxophone
and clarinet. Starting out in the almost unknown Starfighters he then joined
Wild Horses with Brian Robertson (Thin Lizzy), Jimmy Bain (Rainbow), and
Clive Edwards. When UFO called he was only too happy to jump ship or go
from frying pan into fire, depending upon your point of view. It isn't Carter,
however, whose keyboard playing is heard on the album. Former Lone Star
vocalist John Sloman had auditioned for the 'Raymond role', and due to his
late arrival, Carter was restricted to adding backing vocals, and a saxophone
solo.

The album cover, the first by Hipgnosis not to include any pictures of the
band, is another disturbing image featuring a couple, possibly lovers, in a
blurred, colourful haze, the male holding a lit blowtorch. Predictably the

Americans disapproved and the sleeve was toned down for the US release. Similar Stateside objections to the title of the album's final track led to it being shortened to the peculiar 'Profession Of...'.

The Wild was reissued in a remastered CD format in 2009 which included previously unreleased live recordings of 'Long Gone', 'Lonely Heart' and 'Makin' Moves', but no alternative mixes or rejected songs. The album embodies everything that UFO was about; strong, melodic rock songs with uniformly excellent lyrical and musical performances throughout. It is to the band's early 1980s output what *Obsession* was for the previous decade.

Subsequent albums would suffer from less impressive production, misguided tacks in musical direction, and the departure of another key member. There would still be some excellent songs, stellar performances, and impressive live gigs, but an apex had been reached and after *The Wild,* the trajectory was to be generally downwards for the rest of the decade.

'Chains Chains' (Way/Mogg)

Opening with powerful slide guitar and joined by massive, interlocked bass and drums the song shifts into a magnificent grooving riff. Mogg tells his tale of a gambler, Jack of Diamonds, and a dancer, Little Jeannie, both lost souls, and instantly the sound has everything that *No Place To Run* lacked. Here we have attitude, aggression, and integrity.

The sing-a-long chorus is strong and Chapman's solo replicates the chorus melody over the syncopated rhythm part to great effect, rather than cutting loose and possibly spoiling the track. Less, in this case, is definitely more. Subsequent songs would show that the guitarist had lost none of his soloing 'chops'; he is a musician who plays for the song rather than for his ego. A repeated 'Chains, chains' with further tasteful guitar fills bring this classy opener to a natural end.

'Long Gone' (Chapman/Mogg)

'Long Gone' is the album's masterpiece, the best track recorded with Chapman, and sees UFO at their most creatively ambitious since 'Love To Love'. Epic in construction and execution the song is a *film noir* set to music. Mogg depicts a scene of severe urban violence set against the wishes of two nameless lovers who hope to escape the city's nightmare. Lyrically he has never been better, and his vocal performance is spine-tingling and superb.

Opening with a brooding low keyboard drone over which Chapman picks out a simple melody, the lyric instantly paints pictures, 'Skulking in the mean streets, whispered in the halls, red light bandits on the corners, give no quarter calls'. The rhythm section muscle in and the tempo doubles as Mogg becomes even more visceral. The sing-a-long chorus moves into a section with two bars of 7/4 time before switching back to the regular 4/4 signature.

Another fantastic verse lyric, 'Keep on looking for a holy one, some kind of hero or a prophet to come, visionaries dance the night away, there's no tomorrow living for today', is followed by a further chorus, and a descent into Chapman's tortured solo. This finally returns to the atmospheric introduction and Mogg's best lines: 'I saw the stars come out tonight, so lonely and immune, summer rain kissed the streets, that bleed like open wounds...', subtle harmonised keyboards adding to the mood, followed by the relentlessly heavy drive of the final verse, chorus, and the 7/4 section before the song comes to a false ending.

A brief drum fill leads into an extended play-out which is entirely in 7/4 time. A string section create a threatening atmosphere as the guitar, bass and drums fade to nothing, and this micro-symphony comes to a finally calm conclusion.

'Long Gone' is a savage story, told with power, melody, dynamic and textural contrasts. The track has an urgency that conveys angst and passion at every turn, the tasteful inclusion of strings serving only to heighten the drama. And all of this is achieved in less than five and a half minutes. Magnificent.

'The Wild The Willing And The Innocent' (Chapman/Mogg)

The unsettled feeling of 'Long Gone' is maintained in the introduction of the title track as the string section swoop and hover over the simple keyboard and acoustic guitar motif.

The huge, heavy rhythm section pounds in with Chapman adding more excellent slide guitar whilst Mogg is 'looking for a wild rose, in the heat of the night, waiting for a show'. Less lyrically impressive than what has gone before, he is in familiar territory and the song is adorned with classy melodies and harmonies throughout. Propelled by Parker's persuasive percussion, the chorus lyric, 'And the wild, the willing and the innocent, are down down, in the jungle tonight' invites comparisons with the 'Jungleland' chant of 'No Place To Run', with Carter's higher-pitched backing vocals adding further class.

After the standard verse, chorus, repeat structure, the song again returns to its tense opening with Chapman breaking into a solo that reprises the introduction's central melody. Whilst Mogg may have opened his little black book at 'C for Cliché', ('Cold black steel, your last meal, the hand of fate has come'), this remains an intense and compelling number which eventually subsides into a fade of the opening chord sequence with more overlaid strings.

As title tracks go 'The Wild...' is not *quite* in the same league as 'Lights Out' or 'No Place To Run', but it's still a high-quality song with a real sense of atmosphere and purpose.

'It's Killing Me' (Way/Mogg)

A fade in of harmonised guitars cast a Thin Lizzy-esque spell over this downbeat, understated, bluesy groove. Whilst the mood established by the previous two songs has quietened, there is still an inherent tension to this track despite its laid back feel, medium-slow tempo and possibly autobiographical lyrics, 'Living inside a bottle, strung out on a line'.

Way, Mogg and Chapman would all later attest to the early 1980s as being the 'years of excess' which, by their standards, must have been quite something. Inevitably this would take its toll both personally and professionally, but here the words are tinged merely with regret rather than outright bitterness or the evangelical zeal of the newly 'clean'.

The song lifts with its chorus and is even stronger in the bridge section where an organ is prominent. Chapman's solo is another fine example of controlled understatement, restricting his playing to a repeated single line melody with added harmony guitars before returning to the introduction. In the third verse, the string section joins the texture and the chorus is repeated, leading to another harmonised guitar solo which gradually disappears with the chorus as a lush fade. 'It's Killing Me' is the least memorable song on *The Wild* but it is up against some *very* stiff competition.

'Makin' Moves' (Chapman/Mogg)

Whilst 'Makin' Moves' is a relatively straightforward, up-tempo rocker, the arrangements, musicianship, lyrics, and vocal performance lift it into a cruising, riff-based triumph. It begins with a pretty, melodic section with interplay between a violined electric guitar (where a note is struck with the volume off and the sound flowing in to approximate the sound of a bowed violin), piano, and subtle bass.

The song proper starts with a savage, energetic riff (lifted from 'The Fool's Gold' from Lone Star's unreleased third album *Riding High*) and it sounds like Parker kicks his drum kit down a flight of stairs as the rhythm section lock into a class piece of rocking action. Mogg's lyrics depict individual vignettes of characters either struggling to survive, summoning up courage, or to trying to improve their lives despite the passing of time. The refrain 'Yes, I love the way they're makin' moves' is catchy and memorable and after the second chorus, the song reverts to the introduction, this time with the drums maintaining the energy level.

Chapman plays the melody conventionally before breaking into a fast and celebratory solo. A lyrical highlight appears in the third verse, 'There's no silver and there's no gold, it's just that one shot before they're old', and is a theme to which Mogg would return. Repeated chorus refrains and added guitar fills play out as the song fades. 'Makin' Moves' would justly become a concert favourite, and reappeared in the setlist for the band's final tour.

'Lonely Heart' (Chapman/Way/Mogg)

'Mr. Mogg? It's Mr Springsteen's lawyer on the phone again. He says this is really starting to get out of hand now'.

Despite Mogg's denials, the influence is there for all to hear, not that this is necessarily a bad thing. Unless of course, you are a proven songwriter in your own right with an impressive track record of high-quality rock songs to your name.

The lyrics tell the sad story of Sarah unfolding against a backdrop of emotive piano arpeggios. Just as this subtle mood has been established, the guitar, bass, drums and, erm, saxophone destroy the atmosphere. 'Lonely Heart' is a powerful multi-melodic song which drives along effortlessly building to the 'La, la, la, la, la, lonely heart' chorus. Chapman's impressive solo leads back to the piano introduction over which Carter plays a haunting saxophone melody. This is followed by another power-chord blast into the third verse, 'At night you cry yourself to sleep, against the odds you wanted to beat', and after a final chorus the instruments disappear leaving just the piano and mournful interjections from Carter as the music fades away.

I have nothing against the sax in the right context, and here it is supremely effective, especially given the song's obvious homage to 'The Boss'. On the band's next release the instrument would be a *lot* less welcome.

'Couldn't Get It Right' (Chapman/Way/Mogg)
Right from the opening chuggy major key chord riff and tribal drum rhythms 'Couldn't Get It Right' displays its commercial possibilities. The verse is played out in half-tempo with Mogg reflecting again upon the effects of ageing, and the march of time, 'Turn on the radio and it's as dead as the visions dying in your head'.

As the catchy chorus begins, the tempo moves into a double-time feel, 'So now you've got older and the world's got colder than it used to be, every day gets longer, turns into a darker night', before Chapman's solo which again displays restraint and a melodic sensibility designed to serve the song, with the closing bars featuring harmonised phrases. The chorus is repeated, and he plays a busier second solo as the song fades. This poppy rocker was released as a single, backed with a live version of 'Hot 'N' Ready' recorded at the 1980 Reading Festival, and reached number 41 in the UK charts.

'Profession Of Violence' (Chapman/Mogg)
The album's only ballad opens with nylon-strung guitar arpeggios which are soon joined by evocative strings and gentle piano. Lyrically Mogg has been influenced by a biography of the infamous London gangsters the Kray brothers which has the same title, his words being intensely personal, 'Hey babe, what we gonna do, no look behind me glances, straight time, this time we'll take our chances'. This subtle, affecting texture is maintained throughout the second verse and chorus, 'Whisper on the wind, locked in silence, profession of violence'.

The second section of the track is an extended electric guitar solo which places it in the 'Try Me' department of UFO songs with Chapman's distorted tone being joined by bass and drums. This is the only time when comparisons with Schenker are worthwhile, and then only to the extent that what Chapman plays here is just as good as anything his predecessor would have come up with for the same song. His playing is subtle, controlled, melodic, and full of emotion. As the music progresses, the solo becomes increasingly intense, greater in complexity and faster in fingering, dying away after the climactic moments to a single, sustained note of regret. The string section concludes the music with an appropriately minor key chord.

Mechanix

Personnel:
Phil Mogg: vocals
Paul Chapman: guitar
Neil Carter: keyboards, guitar, saxophone, and vocals
Pete Way: bass
Andy Parker: drums
Recorded at Mountain Studios, Switzerland, The Manor Studios, Oxfordshire, Regent Sound, and Maison Rouge Studios, London
Mixed at Media Sound Studios, New York
Produced by Gary Lyons
Released on the Chrysalis label: February 1982
Highest chart places: USA: 82, UK: 8

Mechanix had the potential to be even bigger and better than its predecessor. The new line-up had gelled as a result of relentless touring to promote *The Wild*, Chapman, Way, and Mogg were continuing to prove they were consummate rock songwriters, and the band's live performances remained electrifying. The addition of Neil Carter, and the inclusion of a saxophone as part of the instrumental texture, showed they weren't prepared to sit on any laurels and were looking to broaden their sound whilst maintaining their melodic hard rock roots.

And so the most surprising thing about *Mechanix* is how quickly the musical rot had set in from the heights of *The Wild*. In just a year UFO had gone from greatness to … well, this. Promoting the album Chrysalis placed adverts in the music press claiming 'Mechanix – it will tighten your nuts'. No, it won't. It might leave you with an unpleasant feeling in your stomach, but that will be the sour taste of disappointment.

Whilst the band remained very popular on tour the new album showed significant signs of suffering in the song-writing, musical direction, and production departments. The first and biggest casualty of this debacle was Pete Way who jumped ship in June 1982. Witnessing UFO changing so dramatically and not for the better his departure was both saddening and understandable. He went on to form Waysted and one listen to their debut album, *Vices* (1983), leaves the listener in no doubt as to the direction he wanted UFO to be going in. It's raw, aggressive and full of melodic hard rock energy.

Everything that made *The Wild* so superb is dissipated here. To sabotage an AC/DC album title – if you want mush, you got it. Blame for the flaccid, unexciting, and overly busy sound must be laid firmly at the studio door of producer Gary Lyons. Apparently adopting the mantra 'More must mean better' his mix is awash with synthesizers, and strings appear in an annoying, sickly sweet fashion. Some songs are swamped with backing vocals, and Carter's unnecessary saxophone appears more than once. The overall feel is of 'everything-and-the-kitchen-sink' being thrown around in an attempt to raise

Above: The five alchemists who gave us *Lights Out*, *Obsession*, *Strangers* and, sixteen years later, *Walk On Water*.

Left: Carter, Chapman, Mogg, Way, and Parker about to unleash *The Wild, The Willing, And The Innocent* in 1981.

UFO

Chrysalis

Right: The *Seven Deadly* CD sleeve photo. This was the second Moore-era line-up without a bassist as a full member.

Left: *UFO1*: Some moments of promise but an awful lot of filler. (*Beacon*)

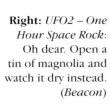

Right: *UFO2 – One Hour Space Rock*: Oh dear. Open a tin of magnolia and watch it dry instead. (*Beacon*)

Right:
Phenomenon:
Schenker arrives,
and the first
proper UFO album
takes flight with
two magnificent
anthems.
(Chrysalis)

Left: *Force It*: True
greatness, and
the cover which
frightened the US
censors. *(Chrysalis)*

Left: *No Heavy Petting*: An absolute belter, if you ignore the cover version. *(Chrysalis)*

Right: *Lights Out*: The long-deserved breakthrough with three out-and-out classics. And some stuff which isn't. *(Chrysalis)*

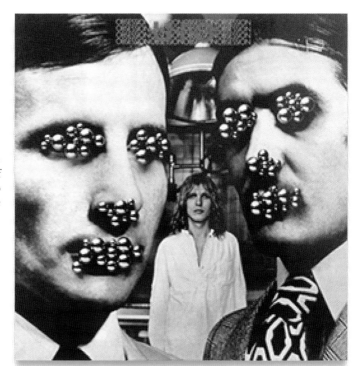

Right: *Obsession*: The apex of Schenker's studio contributions to the band. *(Chrysalis)*

Left: *Strangers In The Night*: Probably the finest live album ever released. *(Chrysalis)*

Left: Mick Bolton. An early low bar for UFO guitarists, playing 'Boogie' on German TV.

Right: Mogg and Parker: Launching 'Doctor Doctor' onto a television audience.

Left: Schenker and Way before the image makeover.

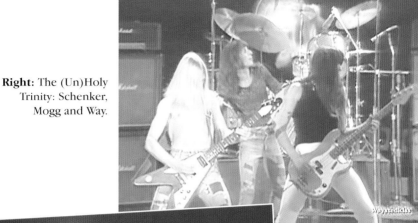

Right: The (Un)Holy Trinity: Schenker, Mogg and Way.

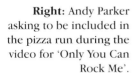

Left: Schenker's legendary concentration on the fretboard meant that sometimes he forgot to put on a shirt.

Right: Andy Parker asking to be included in the pizza run during the video for 'Only You Can Rock Me'.

Left: *No Place To Run*: Schenker out, Chapman in. Producer George Martin manages to sabotage some excellent songs. *(Chrysalis)*

Right: *The Wild…* : The only essential album from the Chapman Era. *(Chrysalis)*

Right: *Mechanix:* Flabby and confused, with far more filler than thriller. *(Chrysalis)*

Left: *Making Contact:* A rubbish sleeve hides a return to form. Sort-of. *(Chrysalis)*

MISDEMEANOR

Left: *Misdemeano*r: Some great songs ruined by an abysmal production and a vast belch of keyboards. *(Chrysalis)*

Right: *Ain't Misbehavin'*: Better than 'Misdemeanor' but hampered by a very rough production. *(FM/Revolver)*

Left: *High Stakes And Dangerous Men*: Mogg and Way join forces with Laurence Archer with some excellent results. *(Essential/Razor)*

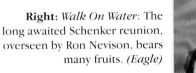

Right: *Walk On Water:* The long awaited Schenker reunion, overseen by Ron Nevison, bears many fruits. *(Eagle)*

Left: *Covenant:* Heavy, hard hitting and polished. An overlooked gem of an album. *(Steamhammer)*

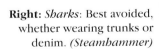

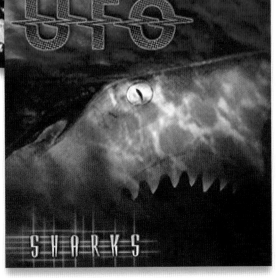

Right: *Sharks:* Best avoided, whether wearing trunks or denim. *(Steamhammer)*

Left: Mogg in *Misdemeanor* mode, 1986.

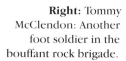

Right: Tommy McClendon: Another foot soldier in the bouffant rock brigade.

Left: Two Pauls: Raymond and Gray share rhythm duties whilst touring *Misdemeanor* in 1986.

Right: Paul Raymond playing 'Love To Love' in Germany in 2005.

Left: Phil Mogg singing 'Love To Love' at the same gig.

Below: The *Last Orders* tour lands in Pennsylvania in 2019 with Neil Carter at the keyboards.

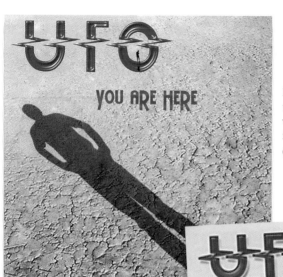

Left: *You Are Here*: Vinnie Moore takes over six-string duties with an impressive first outing from another new line-up. *(Steamhammer)*

Right: *The Monkey Puzzle*: Pete Way's last recorded contribution to the band he formed. *(Steamhammer)*

Left: *The Visitor*: Fantastic cover, terrible album. *(Steamhammer)*

Right: *Seven Deadly* dull songs, the other four are quintessential 'Moore Era' UFO. *(Steamhammer)*

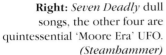

Left: *A Conspiracy Of Stars*: At best you may feel yourself 'whelmed'. *(Steamhammer)*

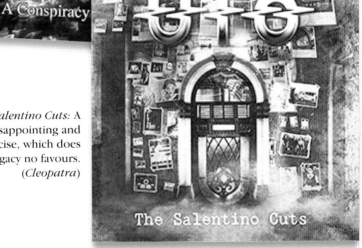

Right: *The Salentino Cuts:* A massively disappointing and pointless exercise, which does the band's legacy no favours. *(Cleopatra)*

Left: *The Chrysalis Years: 1973 – 1979*: A compilation of arguably the best period of the band. *(Chrysalis)*

Right: *The Chrysalis Years: 1980 – 1986*: Another compilation, great in places but the rot had set in. *(Chrysalis)*

Left: *Live Sightings*: A four-CD live package from the Chapman era, plus a rare live LP featuring guitarist Larry Wallis.

the album's game, with failure being very much an option.

Then there are the songs themselves. There are only a couple of really good rockers here, some tracks have a catchy melody or arrangement, but the overall direction appears to be way-out-westward, heading towards the softer, more commercial side of the tracks. The classy, hard-edged, and powerfully mature sound of *The Wild* is gone, leaving this sad husk of the might that once was.

On *Mechanix* Chapman's previously substantial writing contribution is dramatically diminished. He was getting divorced at the time, and the majority of the songs are credited to Carter and Mogg. The vocalist's once ultra-reliable skills seem to be on hold. Some of his lyrics appear to have been written on autopilot and, whilst there is the occasional memorable moment, there is nothing to match the previous year's far superior output. Further evidence of 'Springsteen-ism' doesn't help matters either.

The cover is as uninspiring as the record itself. An 'Eastern Bloc' style propaganda image of a large spanner fitted with a guitar fretboard held in a black leather gloved right hand against a beige background is plain and dull. On the reverse is a small black and white live-action photo of the band amidst the usual information on a blue background.

Mechanix is the low point of the Chapman years. There are just not enough good songs, the overall feel is flat and busy, with far too much going on sonically. Purposeful commerciality has crept in, not enough genuine melodic hard rock is coming out, and the band's integrity seems to have taken the first (mystery) train out of town. The album falls between the two stools of pseudo-American rock and overt commercialisation, neither of which is strong enough to take its flabby weight. This most English of hard rock bands appear only too eager to wrap themselves in the Stars and Stripes, to play average rock music that will satiate crowds but fail to move individual minds.

'The Writer' (Chapman/Mogg/Carter)

Things start promisingly enough with a grinding guitar riff supported by a wash of synthesiser, the chugging rhythm section joins in, and Mogg portrays a tabloid journalist boasting of his power over people's fortunes and reputations. Overall the tempo is on the lazy side, and if the speed had been increased by an extra ten beats per minute, the track would have had a greater urgency and impact. As it is, it feels underpowered and lacking the necessary tension to make a really good opener.

Come the solo section eyeballs roll. Divided into four parts, the first belongs to Carter and his sustained synthesiser. Whilst progress and change are inevitable, and to be welcomed if positive, some things should remain inviolate and a UFO song where the guitar solo is relegated to second billing does not bode well. Worse is to come as the third part is a saxophone solo. Whilst it was effective in 'Lonely Heart', here it comes across as unwelcome and intrusive. Luckily Chapman returns for the fourth section to provide some much needed overdriven relief.

In the final verse, saxophone mixes with guitar on the main riff, whilst in the song's coda, Mogg's repeated 'You're gonna lose' refrains quickly become tiresome. As if realizing this he lurches, bizarrely, into 'So don't you step on my blues suede shoes' as the song fades away with Chapman producing some impressive fills.

'Something Else' (Cochran/Sheeley)

Second song in and it's written by someone else. Terrific, this is just what the album needed. As if to emphasise the beginnings of their decline, UFO's take on the Eddie Cochran standard sounds both desperate and unnecessary. Opening with some heavy-on-the-reverb rhythms, guitar and bass are blended with synthesised choral style backing vocals which are too far forward in the mix. The famously jagged guitar riff is also played by Carter and his seemingly unstoppable saxophone. For the instrumental Chapman delivers the goods but the overall feel of the song is too glossy, being neither aggressive nor committed.

In the fade, Carter blows out with his brass again and by now fans were wondering if this was going to be the soundscape for the entire record. Already, the transition from *The Wild* is both astonishing and disappointing. Where 'Mystery Train' from two years earlier worked superbly, 'Something Else' just … doesn't. Two songs in and anticipation is severely ebbing.

'Back Into My Life' (Way/Mogg)

'Dear Mid-West America, can we have a hit single please?'

Spirits wane further as this overly long, dreary country-ballad-meets-Springsteen stroll-a-long attaches itself limpet-like to the soul. An understated guitar introduction leads into a mid-tempo number, all piano and acoustic guitar as Mogg describes a street scene where everybody is enjoying themselves except the narrator. And listeners to this woeful track. There are some gospel-style backing vocals thrown into the chorus which has little else to recommend it, and whilst Chapman's solo mixes cute country fills with the odd sustained line even he can't rescue this musical car-crash.

The bridge section contains Mogg's best lyrics of the album so far, 'Every shadow's like a ghost who comes and haunts you, angel of the night plays her tricks and stays true'. But by now the texture is overloaded with everything bar the saxophone. Be thankful for small mercies. The final verse idly repeats the first verse with the chorus imploring, 'Won't you please, put a little love back into my life?'. Fans would rewrite the lyrics, 'Won't you please, put a lot more rock into your songs?'. At best, this track sounds like The Eagles having a *very* bad day. The sense of disappointment is now palpable

'You'll Get Love' (Chapman/Carter/Mogg)

And things don't improve with this dull little nonentity, stomping away like a moody child sent to their bedroom. Mogg's tale of a stalker who lives across the hall from the escort he desires is as seedy and downbeat as the tired sounding arrangement. Chapman's solo provides some small degree of relief especially in the melodic chorus progression, but overall this stodgy lump of a track should never have made it onto the album. Worryingly it took three people to write this, and although Mogg's voice soars in the coda section chorus, his words are flat-lining. There's a succinct end, and this unmemorable, going-nowhere-doing-nothing number is thankfully over in fairly short order.

'Doing It All for You' (Way/Chapman/Carter/Mogg)

Finally, things begin to look up, but it's been a long, long wait. Okay, it's only actually been eleven and a half minutes, but it's *seemed* much longer. Starting slowly with powerful drums and crunchy power-chords, the story is of a small-time criminal undertaking one final 'job'. The verse works superbly against the double tempo rhythm, lapsing back into half tempo for the romantic chorus, before cranking it again, 'Tonight we're going to be going out in style'.

There is another expansive chorus before the music moves into a new section, with a superbly sinuous guitar riff over which Chapman's solo is full of angst. The texture thickens with sustained keyboards before falling back into the chorus, which features some gorgeous piano arpeggios, and a return to the power-chords as the double-tempo rhythm carries the song away. Chapman's celebratory sounding solo is submerged in the busy mix leading into a long fade and finally, the album has come to some sort of life.

'We Belong To The Night' (Way/Carter/Mogg)

Fortunately 'side two', as was, is superior to the confusing mess of songs which formed 'side one'. Opening this taut, brisk, uplifting rocker, power-chords fade in over which a heavily phased modulation effect has been added unnecessarily. There are some fast semi-quaver runs which are almost drowned by Lyons' stodgy mix, and when the main riff kicks in there's a reassuring feeling that we're finally back on solid ground as the album's best track gets going.

Mogg's lyrics return to one of his favourite themes, the 'tart-with-the-heart' who wants to escape her situation. Chapman's solo is busy and agitated, going full flight in its final bars as the story returns in the third verse where a sustained synthesiser is added. Carter's backing vocals are strong in the chorus repeats, building effectively to a climactic reprise of the main riff, and then stabbed fading power-chords segue smoothly into...

'Let It Rain' (Way/Carter/Mogg)

The album's most overt single 'Let It Rain' is a poppy, melodic major key number depicting 'Two lovers in a desperate game' with the narrator being 'The married man you laid' who 'goes back home to his own charade'. The juxtaposition of dark subject matter set against a positive musical feel makes for strange bedfellows.

Like a chaotic cook Lyons again can't resist adding too much into the mix, and this time it's synthesised choral voices which are allowed to intrude. Chapman solos against himself in the stereo channels and then we're into repeated choruses never knowing how the saga concludes. The coda section, beginning 'Now you see that love's just a game', leads into some powerful guitar and drum interplay before further catchy choruses with an inevitable fade.

'Terri' (Chapman/Mogg)

Cloying strings underpin the unusual opening to the album's most effective and affecting ballad. Mogg sings of a relationship which is slowly but resolutely reaching a sad conclusion with a world-weary, regretful tone. A cello joins the texture as he reaches the chorus and then the band come in at a reflective tempo providing yet another American country style backdrop to his evocative lyric, 'Every now and then I'd see that wild look in your eyes, it's another long shot that we tried'.

The song builds in the chorus with Chapman's emotive fill-in lines, and the bridge picks up the intensity before a heroic chord sequence leads into the guitar solo. This is followed by a repeat of the chorus and another reflective verse, 'Then I try to phone and swallow my pride, it's no good we tried and tried', before a final chorus. 'Terri' ends on a held, non-tonic chord adding to the ever-present sense of ennui.

A better producer could have turned this into another excellent UFO ballad. In Lyons's fat and clumsy hands, the overblown mix adds unnecessary layers of saccharine as he manages yet again to spoil what might have been. What a talent.

'Feel It' (Way/Mogg)

It's back to Way's World with an archetypal basic, effective chord-based riff which grooves away satisfactorily as Mogg describes the effect a certain woman has on the men of a small-town bar. In the chorus, the melodic factor is increased with harmonised guitar counterpoint before returning to the 'bar and grill' where 'you could cut the air as she walks in'. The chorus has some effective, low-pitched backing vocals which build persuasively into the bridge section, 'Every night she'll make you dream a little more, with a smile that opens every door'.

There is an intense Chapman solo before another verse, 'See her strut she moves from head to toe, and what you ain't got you'll never know'. Further chorus repeats signal the song's ending on another unresolved chord. It says much about the overall quality of *Mechanix* that this reasonable but unspectacular number is one of the album's best tracks.

'Dreaming' (Carter/Mogg)

Luckily, the quality is maintained for this up-tempo driving rocker describing Brighton street gangs allied to a memorably melodic chorus, 'Had a plan we couldn't blow, nobody cares, nobody knows, made a stand and played a show, nobody cares, nobody knows'. The song maintains its hard rock stance especially when Chapman's solo section cuts in, fast and determined. The final section has the chorus repeating several times with Carter's softer voice intoning 'Dreaming' in interchanging left and right channels, and finally taking over from Mogg's vocals as a long slow fade takes us out of the album proper.

It's an energetic conclusion to a record which contains more low points than high and is a sad indication of the decline which long term fans would endure for years to come.

Non-Album Track
'Heel Of A Stranger' (Way/Chapman/Carter/Mogg)
Issued as the B-side to the single 'Let It Rain', this excellent pop-rocker should have been placed firmly on 'side one' to signal some way out of *Mechanix*'s musical morass. Not that anyone was missing it, but Carter's saxophone is back from its holidays and joins the guitar introduction.

'Heel Of A Stranger' is another relationship song, the dispiriting lyrical subject matter again playing out against a joyously brisk major key groove: 'I was seventeen and I thought you were one in a million' and 'At 21 we tied the knot with a holy union' but 'At 29 I realise the dreaming has to end'. The chorus is supremely catchy with a soaring vocal melody. Acoustic guitar and keyboards are added to the mix which leads into a brusque instrumental section, with a new chord progression taking over as Chapman briskly dispatches notes in all directions. There isn't a third verse to conclude the story, but it probably hasn't gone well for the narrator as the song fades on repeats of the chorus.

Put this track up against the unnecessary 'Something Else', the overlong 'Back Into My Life', or the too-dull-to-exist 'You'll Get Love', and it's a mystery why this high energy little number didn't make the final cut. It's hardly the best song the band have ever written, but it's a diamond in the rough compared to a lot of what has preceded it.

Making Contact

Personnel:
Phil Mogg: vocals
Paul Chapman: guitar and bass
Neil Carter: keyboards, guitar, bass, and vocals
Andy Parker: drums
Recorded at The Manor Studios, Oxfordshire, and The Town House, White House
and Maison Rouge Studios, London
Produced by Mick Glossop
Released on the Chrysalis label: January 1983
Highest chart places: USA: 153, UK: 32

Despite Way's departure, the remaining members of UFO gathered their
battered souls again for what would be their last album together. Deciding
against bringing in a new bass player the band still managed to deliver a more
cohesively rocking collection than its lacklustre predecessor.

Mechanix had done well commercially if not critically, and it was initially
agreed that Gary Lyons would be retained as producer. As Lyons's behaviour
had grown increasingly erratic, the band turned to the more disciplined and
professional Mick Glossop and charged him with saving the situation.

The cover looks like one of Hipgnosis's poorer efforts but was credited to
STD/Andrew Ellis. The front image of the back of a naked multi-armed woman
sitting at an old fashioned telephone exchange connecting callers against a
dull gold background is obvious and strained. On the rear of the sleeve, the
newly diminished line-up is shown playing live in a small black and white
photo amidst some suggestive images provided by Hipgnosis main man, Storm
Thorgerson. Inevitably the cover was altered for release in the United States.

Making Contact shows in the main a return to strong melodic hard rock
performed with drive and purpose, four of the tracks being the near-equal of
anything this version of UFO had produced. On the minus side, the overall
sound is too smooth, all of rocks inherent power having been sanded down
and, on more than one track, Carter's keyboards have a constricting effect on
the music. Fortunately this time he has left his saxophone at home.

Mogg's overtly Springsteen influences have been mainly flushed out of his
system and, whilst there are still glances towards America, the album's focus
is mainly back on what they do best. The collection isn't without its duds, but
it's a welcome step up from where the band was a year earlier. *Making Contact*
is a 'dark' album with not enough electric cutting edge to the sound and too
much reverb effect overall. Glossop has, however, managed to bring the band's
sound back to some proper heavy rock and when it kicks, it *really* kicks.

This was to be the final studio release of the Chapman era and the
(temporary) end of UFO. After a series of chaotic European gigs, culminating
with Mogg suffering an on-stage breakdown in Greece, a farewell tour was
mounted for British fans in the spring of 1983. This was partially captured for

posterity and issued as one side of a truly bizarre double album by Chrysalis entitled *Headstone – The Best of UFO.*

Instead of following the thoroughly deserved route of a live album as a fitting tribute, the record label took the head-spinning decision to issue an embarrassing hybrid compilation instead. It included a handful of the band's best studio songs together with tracks by other groups with whom current or former members of UFO had a connection. Yes, it really was *that* convoluted and idiotic. On the fourth side of the twin vinyl package were five songs ('We Belong To The Night', 'Let It Rain', 'Couldn't Get It Right', 'Electric Phase', and 'Doing It All For You') taken from the band's farewell tour recorded at Hammersmith Odeon, London on 15 April 1983 with Paul Gray, formerly of The Damned and Eddie And The Hot Rods, playing bass.

The complete Hammersmith concert eventually emerged as a proper live album in 2009. The band delivers the goods in fine style, producing a worthwhile testament to the end of this particular line-up.

Headstone – Live At Hammersmith 1983
'We Belong To The Night', 'Let It Rain', 'Couldn't Get It Right', 'Electric Phase', 'Doing It All For You', 'Long Gone', 'Chains Chains', 'Lonely Heart', 'Blinded By A Lie', 'No Place To Run', 'Mystery Train'

'Blinded By A Lie' (Carter/Mogg)
Opening with a whoosh of synthesiser Chapman lays down an excellent riff as the band lock into a typical rhythmic groove with an overlaid keyboard melody. After an explosive power-chord, Mogg takes a bitter swipe at the sharp business practices of the band's recently-sacked manager. The song becomes more melodic as it rises after the repeated 'Blinded by a lie's with the laconic lines 'I know it's just the price you pay, I know you're nothing', with excellent interweaving guitar fills. When this section re-appears after the second chorus the slights are extended, 'And oh boy, every dog has his day, I know you'll be the one to pay'.

Chapman unleashes a mighty solo over the 'Lights Out'-style rhythmic backing with some impressive runs and a couple of Van Halen impersonations. The chorus is repeated as the song rolls towards its conclusion with a descending chord sequence slowing into a final power-chord which segues smoothly into...

'Diesel In The Dust' (Carter/Mogg)
...a single repeated bass note with a suitably funky road-dirty guitar riff. The lyrics relate the true story of a notorious bully Ken McElroy who terrorised the town of Skidmore, Missouri for decades, only to be shot dead in July 1981. Re-imagined into a new character, Ted McKinley, Mogg recounts the episode which garnered the town's population to become complicit in the murder and their subsequent silence during the investigation that followed.

The lyricist remains on form with lines including 'McKinley wouldn't back down from any man alive, but you need to if you're to survive'. Again the chorus increases the melodic factor, 'And nobody heard a thing, not a shout or shotgun ring, just the smell of diesel in the dust, diesel in the dust'. After the second chorus, Chapman produces a massively heavy secondary riff which leads into his impressively melodic solo. The third verse concludes the story, 'Just the silence you get from kin to kin' and 'The preacher bowed his head, glad that he was dead, and the better the least that was said', with two further choruses as the song fades into the distance over the throbbing main riff with additional guitar fills, and some peculiar sound effects. Two songs in, both excellent, and things are looking up.

'A Fool For Love' (Carter/Mogg)

And down again. Having given us a bleak American tale with an English hard rock attitude, UFO now once again shift themselves entirely Stateside in a hopeful assault on the singles chart. This melodic poppy rocker opens with strummed chords as Mogg relays his tale of a girl who continually makes bad decisions in her search for love and security. Grooving away in a major key tonality over the verse, the song swings into a more melodic section after the chorus, moving into the relative minor key, and then back into the verse, 'And from sixteen to 32, she lost her loves and her good looks too, it's so sad to see at first hand, from a teenage beauty to a one night stand'.

After the extended second chorus, Chapman's solo starts with single sustained notes slowly building in complexity and intensity until the keyboards rush to the front of the speakers, almost shoving the guitar to one side. The song fades away with repeated choruses, wishing it could be on a Bryan Adams album instead.

'You And Me' (Carter/Mogg)

'...and the awards for 'Worst Ballad On The Album', 'Worst Ballad In The History Of The Band' and 'Most Cloying Use Of Keyboards In A UFO Song' go to...'

'You And Me' is a dreary wade through sonic mud with clichéd lyrics which are almost beyond parody. It is the album's major but not only disappointment, featuring continuously sustained keyboard chords without any space for light and shade. Parker's subdued drumming is the sound of a man slowly mutating into a drum machine. As befits this dreadful track Chapman turns in a merely adequate, mournful solo as Carter continues to put the bored into keyboard.

Words-wise it's the pits, 'Winters' here and it's looking bleak, the snow is falling as we speak'. Lyrically the song concerns a couple going through hard times, with the narrator convinced that no matter what happens to them somehow their love will see them through. Yes, it really is *that* awful. 'You And Me' is blessedly brief, but that doesn't excuse its unspeakable, somnolent dullness, the final keyboard chord segues into...

'When It's Time To Rock' (Chapman/Mogg)

The introduction, which is over a minute long, features a swirling guitar motif played in triplets over booming power chords, drum fills and synthesizer washes. The main guitar riff finally emerges and, given the song's title, it's likely that Chapman and Mogg were trying to write a 'Rock Bottom' for the new decade. 'When It's Time to Rock' is good, but it's definitely not 'Rock Bottom' good. Lyrically Mogg is stumbling around again back in gang territory, and the wannabe anthemic chorus is reasonable musically but embarrassing lyrically, 'When it's time to rock, we're the only ones, no one takes this block, 'cos we're number one'.

After the second verse and chorus, there's some spectacularly heavy guitar riffage before a half tempo instrumental section where Chapman plays an excellent close-miked melody with which he then harmonises. This is followed by a short, grooving riff before an explosive set of fast chord changes and then the song drops back into the main riff for a final verse and chorus. 'When It's Time to Rock' plays out at full tilt with Chapman playing a typically impressive solo as a massive flanged studio effect is added to the substantial fade.

'The Way The Wild Wind Blows' (Chapman/Carter/Mogg)

The first song of the former 'side two' is the last really good track on the album, opening with a sprightly chord sequence before descending into a secondary main riff which sounds similar to 'Pack It Up And Go', albeit at a faster tempo.

The lyrics concern a man on the run from the law due to his relationship with a young woman who turned out to be just a little *too* young, 'Oh, I had Jenny by my side. Oh, she never told me that she lied'. The chorus is classic UFO, committed, muscular and melodic. Chapman unleashes another excellent riff which leads into his solo which, like a lot of his work on *Making Contact,* is not distinct enough in the mix.

Back in the story, the narrator is given an 'eighteen-month rest' by the Judge 'in the county's best', but he remains convinced that Jenny will be there to greet him on his release. The song fades with Mogg singing over himself as the chorus is repeated, and Chapman adding short tuneful lines. Here is an example of the overdone reverb on the album; the song's ending gives the impression of a rock band playing in a cathedral. A 'dryer' sound would have transformed this excellent number into something even more hard-hitting.

'Call My Name' (Carter/Mogg)

The album's second attempt at an American hit single opens with the chorus sung over a church organ keyboard sound. Fears that this could be another disaster along the lines of 'You And Me' prove to be unfounded when 'Call My Name' becomes a distant cousin to 'A Fool For Love'.

A chugging mid-tempo rhythm with a major key set of chord changes makes this an inoffensive, unspectacular piece of pop-rock fodder. The bridge section builds to Chapman's melodic solo although lyrically Mogg seems to be scratching around in the bins again, 'We had nothing to hide, we were just a few years on the wrong side'.

Further choruses presage the fade with the repeated refrain 'There's no shame in our love'. Maybe not, but there is shame in the fact that this song was deemed good enough for inclusion on the album when the single-only B-side track 'Everybody Knows' would have been a far better choice.

'All Over You' (Carter/Mogg)
Things step up a necessary gear with this punchy, tight, stomping rocker. Mogg is back in spiteful form, 'Well you think you're the Queen of Texas, who you fooling now?', as he rails against an unnamed lady who has caused him some unspecified wrong. When it arrives the chorus does not raise the song's game, it just sits in the same key and chord structure, and fails to provide the necessary level of heft.

Chapman's solo section is good with his distinctive soloing style and tone captured far better by Glossop than Lyons' desperately mid-range recordings. 'All Over You' isn't exactly filler, but equally it isn't good enough to be saved from obscurity. Chapman solos over the repeated final choruses and the seemingly inevitable fade. To its eternal credit however, there's one thing 'All Over You' isn't. It isn't 'No Getaway'.

'No Getaway' (Chapman/Carter/Mogg)
In a parallel universe, songs like this and 'You and Me' would never be written, let alone recorded. There is temporary interest in the short, atypical introduction. Some slow, atonal guitar and keyboard arpeggios create an unsettling atmosphere, but this is soon interrupted by, and bears no relation to, Mogg's hopeless first line 'Baby, lives across the street, I know that you're alone'.

It's downhill all the way from there as we're back to a pathetic semi-rehash of the dismal 'You'll Get Love'. This slow stomper is even more useless and has little to recommend it beyond its slight chorus. 'No Getaway' is let down by abysmal lyrics, and a predictable instrumental section where Chapman unsurprisingly fails to find inspiration in the embarrassing words. At times Mogg sounds like a latter-day Big Bopper (of 'Chantilly Lace' fame) insistently wondering aloud why his 'baby' hasn't replied to his correspondence. Why indeed? It's a complete mystery...

There is another instrumental section after the final chorus with Chapman running out of what few ideas he has and resorting to self plagiarisation. Luckily the fade is in sight and it really can't come soon enough for this dull effort performed by a tired sounding band.

'Push, It's Love' (Carter/Mogg)
A manic drum introduction leads into a rising bass riff which is mirrored by the driving guitar. It's strident, bold and promising. And then Mogg starts singing.

If you're okay with 'I'll take you walking out tonight, I'm looking good for you. What you see is what you get, you won't need a cure' then I'm happy for you. But he was coming up with this sort of tosh on *UFO1*. It doesn't get any better, the words expressing various stages of lust.

Musically 'Push, It's Love' is strong, melodic and relentless, especially in the instrumental sections with Chapman working the necessary melodic magic. Lyrically however it sounds thrown together with whatever sprang into Mogg's mind immediately coming out of his mouth. The song ends with the opening riff, short bass interjections and a sudden syncopated power-chord.

Non-Album Track
'Everybody Knows' (Chapman/Mogg)
Released as the B-side to the single 'When It's Time to Rock', this excellent track is another gem in the same vein as 'Heel Of A Stranger'. It should have replaced either 'You and Me' or 'No Getaway', and preferably both.

Opening with a melodically muscular chord sequence, the lyrics chart the relationship between the narrator and a girl who has a secret occupation as an escort, of which he initially has no knowledge. The chorus is catchy and whilst the song follows a conventional structure it has still got more life and attitude to it than a good third of the album from which it was excluded. A return to the introduction welcomes in Chapman's solo, and he also provides a memorable refrain over the fading chord sequence.

Again the elephant in the studio asks 'Why wasn't this on the album?' Digitally of course, it is but, three-plus decades ago a lot more effort was needed to enjoy this slice of high-quality, heavy pop-rock.

Misdemeanor

Personnel:
Phil Mogg: vocals
Tommy McClendon: guitar
Paul Raymond: keyboards
Paul Gray: bass
Jim Simpson: drums
Recorded at The Manor Studios, Oxfordshire
Mixed at Wisseloord Studios, Holland
Produced by Nick Tauber
Mixed and engineered by Jon Jacobs
Released on the Chrysalis label: November 1985
Highest chart places: USA: 106, UK: 74

By 1984 Mogg had recovered his health, relocated to Los Angeles, and had the stage bug again. He sought to leave UFO behind, assembled a fresh band, and went on the hunt for a record contract. Chrysalis was prepared to offer him a deal, but only on the proviso that any new project would still be called UFO. In retrospect, this would prove to be a huge mistake.

Retaining Paul Gray on bass from the final touring line-up of *Making Contact* and re-recruiting Paul Raymond, the search was on for a new drummer and guitarist. Robbie France occupied the drum chair from January 1984 to April 1985, leaving to join Diamond Head. He was replaced by Jim Simpson who had last served as official 'shed-builder' in pomp rockers Magnum. Tommy McClendon had risen to prominence via the 'Spotlight' column in 'Guitar Player', an American magazine. He was one of hundreds of applicants and was handpicked by Mogg who offered him the opportunity, which the guitarist seized with both tapping hands and moved to England.

The musical landscape had shifted since the demise of the *Making Contact* line-up. In guitar terms 'The Shredder' was king. A shredder is a player with incredible speed, usually at the expense of taste and genuine emotion. They would have *really* big hair, a vicious whammy bar style, a heavily distorted tone, and a tendency to sound almost exactly like each other. McClendon was such a guitarist, but he had more to offer, and what attracted Mogg was the musician's ability to write complete songs and arrangements.

A Misdemeanor *(sic)* is defined as a minor wrongdoing, and this album is, therefore, miss-titled as it allowed *serious* musical crimes to be committed in UFO's name, causing significant damage to a hard-earned reputation. Utilising the American spelling of the album's title only served to emphasise the musical focus of this 'new' band.

What upset fans the most upon hearing the new release, was the overwhelming presence of expensive-sounding keyboards. These featured heavily in almost every song, the entire album sounded unbalanced and as 'non-UFO' as it was possible to be. Only Mogg's distinctive vocals reflected the origins of what now sounded like an overtly American commercial rock band. Plenty of groups like this already existed, Night Ranger being just one example among many. The musical world didn't need another, as future sales would attest.

Other problems included the dreadful mid-1980s studio production techniques ('gated' trebly sounding drums, too much reverb) which gave an overall *faux* shine to the sound. *Misdemeanor* is not a pleasant listening experience and, after only a few songs, the whole enterprise becomes wearing and irritatingly predictable. The album comes across as a calculated attempt to crack America's massive 'Adult Orientated Rock' market. With nearly every trace of their British hard rock legacy discarded it was clearly going to be either sink or swim with the masses for this new venture.

There aren't many plusses. *Misdemeanor* has a couple of reasonable melodic rockers and a convincing ballad, but the overall emphasis is so far across the Atlantic it suggests that the band should apply for block American citizenship. Mogg is in fine voice as usual and, on occasion, rediscovers his inventive lyrical skills. But that's about it for the positives.

What the album needed prior to release was a complete re-recording with a producer who understood how UFO should sound, together with a guitarist who wasn't intent on breaking fretboard speed records at nearly every given opportunity.

The album cover was another dud, this time featuring a large colour photo of a teenage girl full of attitude and tattoos, holding a gun. See? Clever! A *'Miss'* with a strange *'demeanour'*. Very good. No, it isn't. On the back, the same girl is gun-less, smiling and sticking her tongue out. There is a small colour photo of the new line-up, all coiffured and looking 'corporate-rock-serious'. None of this boded well.

Six tracks ('Night Run', 'This Time', 'Heaven's Gate', 'Name Of Love', 'One Heart', and 'Blue') were subsequently re-issued as an EP which boasted 'new US remixes'. The differences are minimal. McClendon's guitar tone is slightly better with a greater degree of mid-range and is more front and centre in the soundscape, but fundamentally there is nothing new or exciting to engage the listener. Brace yourselves; we're going in...

'This Time' (Gray/Mogg)

And so the aural assault begins. As a calling card for the rest of the album you only really need to listen to this song. It contains all the elements presented across the other nine tracks; a vast array of different keyboard sounds, an overly bright, ear-grating guitar tone replete with whammy bar excesses, and a horribly-recorded drum sound.

On the up-side, Mogg's voice is in good shape, Gray's bass is sometimes the best sounding instrument, and the (uncredited) backing vocals are of a consistently high quality. 'This Time', like so many of the album's songs, is one of Mogg's relationship lyrics with a catchy commercial chorus. At times the overall sound heavies up but at its weak heart this track is far too keyboard-centric, and so obviously aimed at the radio-friendly side of the American market that any hopes of continuing historical integrity are, ahem, long gone.

'One Heart' (Gray/Mogg/McClendon)

This formulaic tale of a high-class escort is as unexciting as its lyrics, 'One heart stands alone, stripped right down to the bone'. Again keyboards dominate and, after a second semi-anthemic commercial-centric chorus, it's time for McClendon's solo. He opens up his guitar case of clichés and gets out all the toys, whammy bar 'dive-bombs', squeals, incredibly fast runs, and, of course, two-handed tapping. Brilliant. No. Not brilliant. Boring.

There is an opportunity to savour the full awfulness of Simpson's sound in the post solo chorus as the other instruments drop out leaving just vocals and drums. Here is a fine rock drummer at the mercy of a record label and producer who seem intent on making him sound like an expensive drum machine. They succeed.

'Night Run' (Gray/Mogg/McClendon)

An introductory staccato burst of aggressive guitar, bass and drums could mean that things are looking up. A quick check a few seconds in? No, they're not. Raymond's omnipresent, sustained keyboards and another smoothly commercial mid-tempo groove have taken over.

Lyrically Mogg is on thin ice with the opening lines 'Love me tender, love me true, ooh baby what a song could do', and by the chorus, confusion has set in: 'And we have seen the night run, it's a thousand miles away'. Okay…but what is the 'night run', exactly? And how did it manage to 'pass us by in just one day'? At 1.40, In a possibly prophetic moment, Mogg wonders 'Where do you go when you reach the end?' Where indeed?

There is a solo section where McClendon's formulaic fingers bounce all over the fretboard like so many randy rabbits whilst simultaneously fighting for space with multiple layers of keyboards. As with the preceding songs, the chorus is repeatedly repeated and the entire blandness just fades away.

'The Only Ones' (Gray/Mogg)

Question: What's worse than three very similar overtly commercial pop-rock songs back-to-back? Answer: A sluggishly gooey ballad in a similar vein.

As if this wasn't enough 'The Only Ones' is also worryingly similar to the truly dire 'You And Me'. Keyboards again lie over what could have been an interesting track like a gigantic warm marshmallow. A change of texture here could have worked relative wonders if only to relieve the ears from the relentlessly soft, irritating soundscape established so far. Has anyone got an acoustic guitar that Tommy could play?

Words-wise Mogg is showing occasional signs of improvement, 'Last September, it's like yesterday, you slipped through my hands, nothing more to say', and the song acquires a welcome heavier texture in the bridge. McClendon's solo is thankfully more tuneful than flashy and shows melodic skill, but it's his tone which continually irritates. The final chorus repeats four, yes, that's *four* times before the slow fade begins with an arpeggiated melody over the heavy power-chords which had formed the bridge section. It's the best part of the song.

'Meanstreets' (McClendon/Mogg)
This is the album's first proper rocker beginning, controversially, with a guitar riff of some heft. Don't worry, here comes Raymond to smooth things over with his vast polyphonic duvet. Soon 'Meanstreets' becomes a conventional cruise through familiar Mogg territory. The track at least benefits from being heavier and, again, kudos goes to the backing vocals department.

The instrumental contains everything that we have come to expect, a screaming solo with lots of whammy bar dives, and an overwhelming sense of rush. After the final verse and further choruses, the underlying chord progression builds to a climactic coda with a frenetic keyboard solo before coming to a jagged and sudden end. It's the first real rock song on what was 'side one', but that is to damn it with faint praise. If you set the bar low, it's always easy to get over it.

'Name Of Love' (McClendon/Mogg)
Some lengthy keyboard sound effects serve as a sort of introduction before a savage guitar riff starts up which is quickly joined by the bass and drums. The half-tempo restrained verse describes, yet again, a lonely man hoping for love. The more aggressive chorus returns to the original tempo with the unoriginal refrains 'In the name of love is there someone there for me?' and then sadly 'In the name of love, set my heart free'.

The mid-song instrumental section blends keyboards and guitar, which is followed by a helicopter, yes, that's right, a helicopter, taking centre stage in the mix. No, I don't know why either. There's another fast and furious guitar solo, (let me count the ways you can deliver clichés), and the third and final chorus has more overwhelming keyboard flourishes before the song hits the buffers quickly and effectively.

'Blue' (Gray/Mogg)
What starts out as another *Misdemeanor*-by-numbers number has actually got a lot more going for it. Things don't start well as another relationship lyric drops into a clunky chorus, 'Blue, blue, oh baby, where are you? Blue, blue, tell me now, it's not true' But things get better.

The music takes off two minutes in with an anthemic, uplifting major key section culminating in the lines, 'When we stood naked as the fourth of July, a moon shot took off, lit up the sky, the Red Sea was parted for the second time, world at my feet, you were mine, it was...'. McClendon's predictable solo battles again for sonic territory with the keyboards and then moves into a slower, heavier section culminating with the lines, 'The sweetest thing I ever, ever heard, is I will always, always be around'. At this point, Raymond evokes rather than smothers, with a simple atmospheric piano figure and sparse, sustained violin sound before the chorus is reprised. A galloping instrumental coda rounds the song off in impressive fashion. This is much better. Relatively speaking.

'Dream The Dream' (Raymond/Mogg)
And the goodies keep coming. This big country-style ballad starts with more smooth keyboards over what sounds like television dialogue which fades as Mogg finds his muse again with lines including 'Wish I could see the blazing sunset, falling right into the bay, but I'm a long time gone, a long time gone'. His vocal tone and phrasing are as good as anything he's produced before, and the huge chorus elevates the song to another level musically if not lyrically.

Sadly the quality level drops for the trite commercial bridge section, 'Lonely days, lonely nights...' and then McClendon produces a relatively restrained and yet still horrible sounding solo. After the third chorus, there are some pretty, harmonised guitar lines and the song fades after its fourth chorus.

Whilst this is a big 'American' ballad, it is also a highly effective piece of music with an epic scope to it. Following the earlier disappointments these three songs, despite the ever-present sound and production irritations, are strong and more compelling.

'Heavens Gate' (McClendon/Mogg)
An agitated guitar, bass and drums-in-unison opening bodes well, but the music soon relaxes into another mid-tempo, keyboard dominated groove which only heats up when the chorus arrives, 'I can't wait for you, heaven's gate won't wait'.

The instrumental builds tunefully into a flashy display from McClendon who banishes any thoughts of taste or phrasing and just throws everything he's got at the underlying chord sequence. At 2.40 a new atmospheric section has Raymond providing another effective interlude before a return to the repeated chorus. The coda reprises the powerful introduction as the song ends on a sustained non-tonic chord.

'Heaven's Gate', again, has decent rock potential, but the inherent songwriting quality is swamped by the omnipresent keyboards and production failings.

'Wreckless' (McClendon/Mogg)
This song describes careless behaviour, a 'gung-ho' attitude, and should really have been called 'Reckless'. This is the throwaway party number to conclude the album, although it starts as a ballad with reflective vocals over modulated guitar strums. Joined by the bass and drums for the chorus the song kicks up

a gear at 1.10 and moves into an up-tempo 12/8 rhythm with some welcome energy.

This is an ode to having a good time for just one more weekend, although there is an underlying sense of ennui in Mogg's delivery. McClendon's guitar is gritty, the keyboards are relatively unobtrusive, and the whole thing grooves along nicely into a melodic bridge section.

The inevitable guitar solo is as emotionally dull as it is technically spectacular. In his own way, McClendon's solos are as boring as Mick Bolton's, both musicians being so intrinsically sucked into the clichés of their particular style and period. After a second bridge section and a final chorus, the song comes to a tight end.

Non-Album Track
'The Chase' (McClendon/Mogg)

This disposable, utterly predictable track was the B-side to the album's first single, 'Night Run'. The verse is desperately dull, although the chorus lifts matters very slightly. It's just not good enough though, even by this album's startlingly mundane standards.

The best moments are in the instrumental section after the overly-busy guitar solo which sits over a half-decent chord riff. The music moves into a tight, triplet based rhythm, with military-style phased drums, and sustained guitar notes creating a suitably different feel.

But that's it. I can find nothing else positive to say about this song. The chorus repeats, and repeats, and nobody cares as the song fades away to even greater obscurity than the rest of *Misdemeanor*, an album which saw UFO (in effect, Mogg and some hired hands) abandon their innovative hard rock roots and try to imitate the corporate success of less talented musicians in a vain attempt to get on the big money train.

Ain't Misbehavin'

Personnel:
Phil Mogg: vocals.
Tommy McClendon: guitar and backing vocals.
Paul Gray: bass.
Jim Simpson: drums and backing vocals.
Guest musician:
David Jacobsen: keyboards (uncredited)
Recorded at The Abattoir and SSE Studios
Produced by Neil Levine
Mixed and engineered by Alan Cave, John Shaw and Neil Levine.
Released on the FM/Revolver label: February 1988
Highest chart places: Did not chart

The re-launch of UFO as an American 'AOR' band, with pomp-rock accoutrements, didn't go down well in its target market, or back home in the UK. Sales were unspectacular, fans felt betrayed, and during the American leg of the subsequent tour, Paul Raymond left again. The band was dropped by Chrysalis and, armed with this demo-rough stop-gap of a mini-album, Mogg once again sought a new record contract.

In a straight fight between the two McClendon albums *Ain't Misbehavin''* wins out over its nadir of a predecessor every time. Putting aside the low budget production here, the arrangements are dominated and driven by guitar. Adopting a smoother more mid-range tone, McClendon's musical flair, although still derivative, shines through in a better balanced if low rent mix. Keyboards are used in a supportive rather than suffocating role, and the songs themselves display more melodic muscle and attitude than the corporate, confusing mess that was *Misdemeanor*.

To assuage fans' very real concerns that UFO was now predominately just a keyboard based band with a side order of flashy guitar solos, this collection should really have been called *Ain't Misdemeanor*. The whole enterprise has an energy about it that, with serious backing by a record company, would have produced a much better album than *Misdemeanor* had been under Chrysalis's constrictive control.

The down-market cover is a medium-sized pencil drawing by Brian Downey of a naked woman sketched side on from the neck down to her waist holding a pistol. On the reverse are numerous in-the-studio colour photos of the band.

This new project didn't do well enough to attract major label support and the band split up again. As a result, *Ain't Misbehavin''* was the final original UFO product to be issued in the 1980s, a decade which had started with so much promise before the continual pressures of work, success, substance abuse, and misguided changes of musical direction, resulted in this budget collection of under-produced tracks for a small label. It was a short, sad, untidy epitaph for a once-legendary band.

'Between A Rock And A Hard Place' (McClendon/Mogg)

Emphasising the cheap nature of this mini-album, 'Between A Rock And A Hard Place' commences after McClendon has begun playing in the studio. Mogg could well be summarising his personal and professional situation in the opening lines of this chugging rocker, 'I'm feeling static, nothing's moving here for me, dead unromantic, that's the way life's squeezing me'. The bass and drums join in on a tight groove with McClendon laying down some spacious chord arpeggios. The song becomes heavier as it moves into the chorus with Mogg adopting a tough guy persona, and the inherent energy here compared to the majority of *Misdemeanor* is palpable. They sound like a proper rock band, albeit a poorly recorded one.

After the second chorus, the bridge ups the power factor further before McClendon launches into his solo where the words 'Van' and 'Halen' quickly spring to mind. Here at least he is playing with a greater melodic sensibility and a more listenable rock guitar tone. After repeated choruses, there is a section where just vocals and drums feature (compare and contrast with the same trick pulled on 'One Heart'), and the song cruises to a fade.

'Another Saturday Night' (Grey/Mogg)

Early ballad warning! 'Another Saturday Night' isn't as good as 'Dream The Dream', but it remains a full-blown, mid-tempo number with an edgy, rhythmic structure over which Mogg lets loose about searching for 'a real love' instead of 'just another Saturday night'.

Subtly placed keyboards seek to enhance rather than smother the song. By the time the bridge section arrives, there is a suspicious waft of *Misdemeanor* in the air except now the music is heavier. McClendon's solo has many predictable elements to it, but he is also putting in more melodic phrases and allowing greater space in his playing. The song builds well to the final choruses, with a reprise of the introduction and an additional solo before finishing on a single held chord.

'At War With The World' (McClendon/Mogg)

Well, not the world, just one man actually. And this man is the cause of Mogg's disquiet as his lady has been cheating on him with an unidentified lover. The funky, upbeat riff doesn't rescue some dreadfully clichéd lyrics, 'Cuts me like a knife' isn't exactly cutting edge in its originality.

Come the chorus the backing vocals add class and the melodic instrumental section features harmonised guitars to good effect, leading into a reprise of the introduction. There is a production blooper as the track fades; just when the overall volume is close to zero, the song actually comes to a clumsy if very quiet finish.

'Hunger In The Night' (McClendon/Mogg)

A steady, up-tempo drum rhythm sets up this terribly titled song, over which the spectre of the then-fashionable 'Hair Metal' scene hangs. Numerous albums by second rate groups of the era had tracks with titles like this. Yes, Dokken, I'm thinking of you. Mogg could and should do better. The story, such as it is, lives down to its name. The protagonist may be a voyeur, a stalker, or maybe much worse.

The opening lyrics set a good first impression, 'There's a half-light of a neon moon in the darkness of this shuttered room' and the chugging guitar rhythm move the song effectively into the chorus. The bridge section, coming as anticipated after the second chorus, is banal, and McClendon produces a suitably fast, agitated solo into repeated choruses.

There is a further guitar solo as a play-out, and the number fades away, no doubt into 'the night', its implied evil still to be unleashed. Or not. I'm really not bothered either way. Lyrically awful, musically energetic with a real sense of commitment, this is a frustrating song which would have been so much better with entirely different words.

'Easy Money' (McClendon/Mogg)
There's a risible, half-shouted phrase over the lush opening distorted chord sequence, 'Let's go, while we're young'. Phil, mate, you were 40 years old when this was recorded.

The rhythm picks up into another steady rhythmic chug, and lyrically we're in the world of the minor underworld dweller, a small-time criminal who is shifting 'easy money' with a 'dozen complications'. He is caught in a reality full of 'sticky situations and a woman's revelations', although Mogg never actually goes into any details. After the second chorus, there's a bridge section with prominent keyboards and heavy power chord blasts. A brisk and frenetic guitar solo follows with more choruses replete with resolute backing vocals to the fade.

'Rock Boyz Rock' (McClendon/Mogg/Simpson/Grey)
There is a nod to 1970's glam rock band Slade here, especially with one line in the intellect-dodging chorus, 'C'mon baby, feel the noise'. 'Rock Boyz Rock' is an upbeat, major key groover which has a similar 'party' feel to the emotionally lightweight 'Wreckless'.

The solo section contains more impressive homages to Van Halen then McClendon manages to become more individually melodic. A repeated chorus section leads into the sub-moronic chant 'Rock boys rock', where there is 'no room for a compromise'. There never is in Cliché World. An upward key shift with more repeats of the chorus signals the approach of the ending, which is clumsily executed.

Non-Album Track
'Lonely Cities Of The Heart' (McClendon/Mogg)
Not issued as part of the original three songs-per-side vinyl, 'Lonely Cities of the Heart' appeared as the final track on the subsequent CD release. This light

rock number is intriguing. It contains gritty, sparse guitar, and plenty of overall melody as Mogg describes a night-time scenario, an 'urban landscape' from which he wants to escape to become a better man than his father. The chorus lyrics are again clichéd and dull ('Living in the lonely cities of the heart, hiding in the shadows, waiting in the dark'), despite the backing vocals.

McClendon's overly energetic solo is set against some staccato rhythms, and the bridge section contains the memorable couplet, 'I can take a little pain, but not tonight again'. The song moves into its third verse which is instrumentally sparse and consequently more effective with a single sustained violin line adding atmosphere. There are further choruses which, strangely, feature a vibraslap in the percussion arrangement, and then this mostly superior song ends with McClendon tapping out some subtle single notes in the fade against some synthesiser phrasing.

High Stakes And Dangerous Men

Personnel:
Phil Mogg: vocals
Laurence Archer: guitar, backing vocals
Pete Way: bass
Clive Edwards: drums
Guest musicians:
Don Airey: keyboards
Terry Reid, Stevie Lange, and Nic Holland: backing vocals
Recorded at Livehouse Studios, Launceston, Cornwell, Studio 125, Burgess Hill,
Black Barn Studios, Woking, and Wessex Studios and EZ Studios, London
Produced by Kit Woolven
Released on the Essential/Razor label: February 1992
Highest chart places: Did not chart

After nearly four years without a sighting, the fifth incarnation of UFO took flight. Having re-established contact in 1988, Way and Mogg were keen to return to their hard rock roots and started writing songs with a view to putting a new band together. This could have been an opportunity to re-recruit Paul Chapman, who had served alongside Way in Waysted from 1984 till 1987 at a time when they sounded more like UFO than UFO did. Paul Raymond, having played with both Michael Schenker (*MSG* -1981), and Waysted (*Vices* – 1983) was also available.

Instead, initially working with Fabio Delrio on drums and going through a variety of new guitarists (Mike Gray, Rick Sanford, and Tony Glidwell), during the period 1988 to 1990, finally two new players were added to the band's family tree: Laurence Archer, formerly of Stampede and Phil Lynott's Grand Slam, and the well-regarded Clive Edwards who had played with Wild Horses, *inter-alia*.

Archer is a fine guitarist whose style and sound is closer to Schenker than Chapman. Fortunately, he is a long way away from McClendon and, whilst elements of 'shredder' technique feature (yes, there is occasional whammy bar usage, yes, there is some two-handed tapping), these are only deployed when the song requires it. Archer's contribution to UFO's return-to-some-degree-of-form should not be underestimated, and Edwards's excellent drumming drives all the songs along with precision and power.

Given the band's diminished reputation there was little on offer from record companies. Mogg and Way were justifiably seen as a risk and, with nearly a decade since UFO's last semi-decent album, *Making Contact*, this was an understandable attitude. Producer Kit Woolven, who had a strong track record via his work with Magnum, Thin Lizzy, and Wild Horses, was hired to oversee the album's production.

The economies of the new deal extended to the cover design which merely featured a large UFO logo imposed over an appropriately stormy sea, with the album title at the sides. The inner pages had four individual photos of the new line-up although clearly, the budget didn't run to more than one chair and a single large spider's web backdrop. There were no additional pages for the lyrics and the song titles were listed on the rear of the insert.

Overall *High Stakes* is a solid, consistent, melodic rock album which moves defiantly back towards what Mogg and Way do best. There is a greater blues influence than has been heard previously and, although the album lacks any lasting 'classic' songs, there are certainly no duds either. It's a rewarding listen and whilst some tracks have echoes of former glories, others sound new, fresh, and determined.

'One Of Those Nights' was issued as single backed with 'Ain't Life Sweet', and a new version of 'Long Gone', which dispensed with the orchestration, is faster than the original, and ends with a frantic guitar solo. Unsurprisingly it failed to chart.

A subsequent live album *Lights Out in Tokyo-Live*, recorded in June 1992, included Jem Davis on keyboards and featured:
'Running Up The Highway', 'Borderline', 'Too Hot To Handle', 'She's The One', 'Cherry', 'Back Door Man', 'One Of Those Nights', 'Love To Love', 'Only You Can Rock Me', 'Lights Out', 'Doctor Doctor', 'Rock Bottom', 'Shoot Shoot', 'C'mon Everybody'

Perhaps inevitably, this version of the band was not to last. During a gig in St Petersburg, a drunken Mogg fell off the stage and broke his leg. In one moment all the hard work that had gone into re-establishing UFO as a serious proposition was in danger.

In addition, there was the constant background clamour from fans demanding a reformation of the *Strangers* line-up and, aware that the mood was moving against them, Archer and Edwards quit the band. Mogg and Way had been in communication with Schenker over the years and the stage was now set for what many had thought would never occur again.

'Borderline' (Way/Mogg)
Opening with the sound of a passing heavy goods vehicle, 'Borderline' describes the life of a contraband smuggler. Over a relentless hi-hat rhythm, Archer's blues fills and tasteful slide guitar lead into a heavy verse riff culminating in a big melodic chorus, 'One step closer to the Devil, one step further from the law, I guess I'm just on borrowed time, one step closer to, one step closer to the borderline'.

Archer's first solo is fast and fluid and returns to the quiet introduction before another verse/chorus combination with Mogg in strong voice. The final solo contains a magnificent, flowing run of overlaid triplet notes which recalls Schenker at his best, and the track ends subtly with a brief reprise of the subdued opening. The first track of the new album contains all the necessary characteristics of *High Stakes*; excellent guitar playing front and centre, superb vocals, interesting lyrics, a rock solid rhythm section, and an almost complete lack of keyboards.

'Primed For Time' (Archer/Mogg)

The introductory riff sounds like an AC/DC out-take with its off-beat drum and bass stabs. 'Primed For Time' soon settles into a groove, breaking out into another melodic chorus, 'It's a nervous breakdown, a teenage shakedown, a nervous breakdown, just one of those things'. The sustained keyboards support the song as it shifts key upwards into Archer's solo which features some furious wah-wah pedal abuse.

This new band sound almost as good as the Chapman version did with *The Wild*, polished, powerful and confident. It's as if the last ten years had never happened.

'She's The One' (Archer/Mogg)

What initially sounds like a ballad soon broadens into an enjoyable enough rock track with a pop edge. A simple drum rhythm is joined by subtle guitar arpeggios and tasteful keyboards over which Mogg's restrained verse soon leads into a full-throated chorus.

Archer's solo plays out over a different chord progression which is more akin to a bridge section in the song's structure. 'She's The One' builds effortlessly into a reprise of the chorus before coming to a calm ending, which is preferable to the anticipated 'fade on the chorus' option.

'Ain't Life Sweet' (Mogg/Way/Archer/Edwards)

The best track on the album opens with a twisty guitar riff, Mogg's interjection ('Ow!') and, bizarrely, a cigarette lighter being lit. This driving, bluesy rocker moves at a terrific pace with Archer adding occasional slide guitar. The sardonic refrain, 'Ain't life a treat, ain't so sweet, when you're down on down, down on down', is followed by a possibly autobiographical reference, 'The bank's foreclosing in and there's a freak sign on my door, the telephone's not ringing, and I can't take it anymore'.

Mogg makes an amusing pre-solo comment, 'Hit me Shorty'. Archer is considerably taller than Mogg but then again, so are a lot of people. The solo is excellent, culminating in a few shredder-esque moments, and the song comes to a stuttering end with more slide guitar. Four songs in and its all good so far. *High Stakes* may not be *The Wild*, but it's certainly no *Misdemeanor* either.

'Don't Want To Lose You' (Way/Mogg)

Oh dear. First thoughts are that this is a remake of the dire 'Back Into My Life' with its 'country-meets-soft-rock' feel. The mix of acoustic guitar and rim shot drumming is effective, and fortunately, the power comes in shortly afterwards soon dispelling any worries of an impersonation of one of the band's weakest tracks.

Lyrically Mogg is still painting good pictures; 'Money goes like a wino's skin, slips through my hands', and some excellent backing vocals feature in the chorus which sags with the repeated 'Don't want to lose you' refrain. More layers of instrumentation are added, and Archer's solo is suitably melodic and sparse as the song builds again into further choruses.

This is where the number starts to get tiresome. It's the longest and least involving track on the album, and could easily have been cut by over a minute without losing any of its value. This wouldn't have made it much better, just shorter, and the inevitable fade is very welcome.

'Burnin' Fire' (Way/Mogg)
A pumping bass and rim-shot drum rhythm are overlaid with tasteful bluesy guitar and controlled feedback giving this song a ZZ Top feel which turns into a typical mid-speed stomper. Mogg's lyric tells the tale of a preacher who becomes tempted by 'God's own creature' leading to his downfall, 'I jumped in to the burnin' fire, led by lust and my desire'. Whilst rhyming 'fire' with 'desire' isn't exactly breaking new ground, the combination of Mogg's soulful tone and the strong backing vocals add real weight to this song. Archer's tasteful solo is short and snappy and is followed by a quieter verse and chorus before building into louder repeated choruses and a predictable rock ending.

'Running Up The Highway' (Way/Mogg)
This upbeat rocker opens with duelling guitars before slipping effortlessly into a familiar rhythm which doesn't let up until the end. The lyrics compare the dreams of a man wanting to be in a successful band with the realities, 'Since I signed up, I've been living in a trance' and 'I've got marines marching through my head'. Again the backing vocals strengthen the sing-a-long chorus.

In the second verse, Mogg references both ZZ Top ('TV Dinners, well I love that band'), and Iron Maiden ('If you see Eddie just say 'Hi''.) There is another impressive guitar solo which adds class to this straight-ahead boogie number followed by the last verse and chorus, and a final rapid-fire solo to a solid finish.

'Back Door Man' (Archer/Mogg)
'Back Door Man' is a slow, menacing heavy blues number with an air of 'On With The Action' about it with its bleak subject matter, and oppressive musical atmosphere. The subdued verse lays the ground, 'Your worst nightmares rolled in one, I'll find you sure as the rising sun', and 'Don't make a noise, it's understood, this ain't no story like Red Riding Hood'.

Mogg inhabits the mind of a troubled individual, and the mood darkens further when the opening riff becomes the titular chorus. The brooding feel never lets up the pressure and Archer unleashes two excellent solos during the number, with his contribution in the coda section being particularly effective in-between Mogg's 'Back door man' refrains. An impressive long run of notes finishes the song off over the final hanging chord.

'One Of Those Nights' (Way/Mogg/Archer)
A soft keyboard and smooth guitar introduction briefly fool the ears into potential ballad territory. When the rhythm section kicks in and the volume

increases 'One of Those Nights' becomes closer to 'Young Blood' in spirit. This is another of Mogg's regretful romance songs with the chorus 'Was it just one of those nights, something I don't remember' hitting the required commercial spot.

Archer's solo has echoes of Chapman's style and the song finishes after repeated choruses with some interesting chord arpeggios. 'One Of Those Nights' is an adequate but un-involving song, although musically there's plenty of highly proficient playing to be enjoyed.

'Revolution' (Way/Mogg)

This is another simple chord sequence and predictable rhythmic number. Edwards mimics some of Andy Parker's drum fills in the introduction before the song settles into another mid-tempo chugger that sounds suspiciously familiar.

The better quality chorus, 'This will be my own revolution, a burning flag held high, I will make my own constitution, till the day I die', leads into a bridge section which returns to the choruses with the excellent backing vocals. Edwards provides further Parker-inspired fills as the song fades. Whilst 'Revolution' and 'One Of Those Nights' have echoes of earlier UFO tracks the next song really goes for it in the tribute stakes.

'Love Deadly Love' (Way/Mogg)

Opening with a mixture of country styled piano, hi-hat rhythm and guitar fills, this song soon explodes into 'Son-Of-Lonely-Heart' with a familiar underlying rhythm borrowed, yet again, from 'Lights Out', and Mogg's 'Sha-la-la, it's not over till it's over' chorus lines. All that's missing is a saxophone. Fortunately, Archer doesn't play the instrument and instead steps into the gap with another melodic, squealing solo which saves the song from outright self-plagiarisation.

There is, of course, nothing wrong with playing to your strengths and 'Love Deadly Love' is full of energy and attitude. However, once we get to 'Never say no, never say no, no, no, no' (4.16) using the same vocal melody and chord sequence as 'Lonely Heart' (3.40) then it's fair to say things have gone too far.

'Let The Good Times Roll' (Archer/Mogg)

A loose underpowered riff with overlaid lead fills falls into another unexceptional medium speed rocker which contains just about enough contrast in the instrumentation to keep interest up. The tempo feels too slow, and the song lacks sufficient energy as a consequence.

In the chorus, the backing vocals again add class, and although Mogg's performance is, as ever, high quality, this final number smells of filler. Archer pulls off another exemplary solo and his playing at the close is just as good, as the song comes to its punchy end.

Walk On Water

Personnel:
Phil Mogg: vocals
Michael Schenker: guitars
Paul Raymond: keyboards and guitar
Pete Way: bass
Andy Parker: drums
Guest musicians:
Mark Philips, Denny Godber: backing vocals
Recorded at Rumbo Recordings, Canoga Park, California
Produced by Ron Nevison
Released on the Eagle label: April 1995
Highest chart places: Did not chart

Whilst *High Stakes* was a definite improvement on what had passed for UFO since 1985, what the fans really wanted to see was a reformation of the *Lights Out-Strangers* line-up. Although the Chapman era had provided plenty of great songs, many felt that the true essence of UFO was in the chemistry between Schenker, Mogg, Way, Raymond and Parker, and demands for a return to the 'glory days' were never far away.

Money was going to be a factor in any reformation. UFO never had any problem spending it, and decades of poor management, plus excessive studio bills meant they never had much of it. With significant financial backing from Japan and a record deal with Zero Corporation, the 'classic' line-up reassembled with a huge weight of expectation on their shoulders. Would they be as good? Yep, pretty much. Would they produce an album to match the 'Golden Trio' of *Lights Out*, *Obsession* and *Strangers*? Almost. Could they hold it together? Seriously?

The band's strategy was to ignore *everything* that had occurred post-*Strangers* and to come back with 'business as usual', both on record and tour. Neither Schenker in his various solo guises, nor UFO without him, had achieved greater critical or commercial success than either could realise through working together. And they all knew it.

Mindful of the fact that his name would always be linked to the early success of the band Schenker negotiated a 50% ownership of the name. In effect, UFO could not operate as 'UFO' without Schenker being involved as an active member. This would have significant ramifications on tour as the German's volatile personality led to no-shows, gig cancellations, and frustrated fans.

Notwithstanding this, *Walk On Water* is an excellent album and is worthy of the 'continuation' crown the band sought. The first three tracks would feature on subsequent tours and, whilst none of the new songs would quite reach the lofty heights of the best of the 1970s output, all are strong examples of high quality, melodic hard rock. Although all the promotional activity stressed that the band was taking up enthusiastically where they had left off, fans were inevitably wondering just how long it could last. It didn't, of course, but what remained was the music with all its integrity and power and this, in the long run, was what mattered most.

Walk On Water delivers. There are no instrumentals, no string orchestrations, and no dud tracks. This is a straight-ahead rock collection with Nevison's crystal clear production once again focusing on the band's strengths of melody, arrangement, and dynamic variation. There is an undeniable musical chemistry between Schenker and Mogg, the majority writers of the album. Mogg's vocals sound as good as ever. Lyrically the album has a recurring theme, the progress of time and the struggle to remain true to what was important to you when you were younger. Aside from a couple of clunking moments, his words are, as usual, skilfully effective. Schenker's tone is bright and aggressive, his soloing is, on occasion, stunning, and his overall contribution to the album is consistently impressive.

Walk On Water contains no cover versions unless you include the unusual step of the band covering two of their own songs. Ignoring the adage 'If it ain't broken...' the surprising decision was taken to re-record 'Doctor Doctor' and 'Lights Out'. It was felt that having modern updates of two classic songs from the first Schenker era would provide a link to the band's past. This was nonsensical. Given the extended running time of CDs compared to vinyl what fans actually wanted was more new songs, not retreads of a past they already possessed. Both song titles were suffixed with '95' to differentiate them from their two-decade-old counterparts.

Of the pair 'Doctor Doctor 95' fares better, with the introduction featuring evocative piano arpeggios, and Schenker's 'seagull-cry' fills. In the song itself, there are plenty of interweaving lead guitar lines, and harmony backing vocals on the 'Livin', lovin'' refrains. It's good to hear the texture beefed up with Raymond's organ contribution and the *Phenomenon* fade is replaced with the more creative, and now standard, *Strangers* ending.

'Lights Out 95' is slightly slower, sounds vocally forced, and is virtually a carbon copy of the original with an updated sound. Schenker again throws in the odd effective smooth line throughout the verses, but it's the same line-up with the same producer playing the same song, so there's nothing more interesting or better executed than in the original, the only change of any significance being again the 'live-stop' coda. It would have been better to hear one of the pre-Nevison songs given a modern reboot.

Differing versions of the CD booklet exist. Mine is unspectacular, looks cheap, and shouts 'Bootleg!'. The band, all dressed in black with Schenker in the middle sporting a hat, stand in front of a large green and slightly fuzzy UFO logo against a dark blue background, their images reflected in the shallow water they are standing on. Inside is an improvement with the inclusion of the song lyrics in the multi-page booklet and better quality photos of the individual members.

'Self Made Man' (Schenker/Mogg)

An atypical, atonal Schenker riff opens this highly anticipated new collection with a mid-tempo rhythm kicking in. Mogg's savage lyrics delve into the mind of a businessman aligned with the right-wing values of Thatcherism, 'A greedy, nasty, selfish little man, who can never have or get too much' who will 'change the course of the river and never stop to count the cost'. Biting and spiteful, his vocals and words are first class. Dropping into a half-tempo bridge section which includes an unusual reggae-style rhythmic backing, the music then accelerates back to tempo for the exhilarating chorus complete with backing vocals.

The instrumental break is in three sections. Initially, there is a cheery-sounding, short double-tracked guitar refrain which then moves into a low-register melody over a continuous two-chord pattern played out in four-bar phrases. The keyboards add to the atmosphere which becomes much darker with a malevolent section in half-tempo. Sardonic laughter is heard way back in the mix and Nevison has placed plenty of reverb here to heighten the tension. Interspersed with Schenker's sparse, brutal phrases and controlled feedback over a heavy, doom-laden riff, there is then a return to the introduction and the verse/bridge/chorus structure.

The main guitar solo swoops and soars magnificently over a minute long fade of the chorus's underlying two-chord sequence. Raymond's keyboards, which have played a subtle, supporting role throughout the song, grow in presence as the track fades. 'Self Made Man', whilst not being in *quite* the same league as most UFO album openers, is a solid, melodic hard rocker with plenty to provide evidence that they were back.

'Venus' (Schenker/Mogg)

If fans were in any doubt whether the reformed band could still deliver the goods, 'Venus' provides an unequivocal 'Yes'. Mixing melody, dynamics, evocative lyrics and a spiralling guitar solo it is quintessential UFO.

Opening with some church organ chords, the song soon into action with a balanced blend of acoustic and electric guitar rhythms. The verse is back to just acoustic guitar with Mogg examining the lure and hold of the Goddess of Love, 'Has her blackness touched your very heart? She'll smile sweetly as your world falls apart'. The rhythm kicks back in, leading to the sing-a-long refrain, ('Oh no, it's such a cold, cold feeling'). The song moves into a strong, melodic bridge section with an effective counterpoint between guitar and keyboards before the organ chords preface Schenker's excellent solo. There is another verse, ('Waves of darkness rise like the sea, in her addiction I will drown'), and refrain, before leading into a faded play out with Schenker simply flying.

'Venus' is UFO back yet again at the height of their collective game, and is a modern companion to classics like 'Out In The Street' and 'I'm A Loser'.

'Pushed To The Limit' (Schenker/Mogg)

This storming rocker should have opened the album, although the tempo is on the steady side. Those of us who witnessed the song live heard a much more energetic and dynamic interpretation, which was captured on the live release *Werewolves Of London* recorded in, erm, Wolverhampton in February 1998.

Lyrically Mogg is raging against the dying of the light, a determination not to give in to the march of time. There is a defiant confidence to his delivery matched by the song's unrelenting pace and power, and as ever melody is never far away, the bridge section having a lighter, pop feel to it.

Schenker delivers two astonishing fluidly fast solos, one in the middle of the song, one towards the end. After a reprise of the chorus, there is a brief, wonderful dual guitar and keyboard fill in two bars of 7/4 time, before returning to the main riff and another verse. This is the first example of Mogg's penchant for obscure, inherently English references, 'My Dad's an angry man, sometimes like Desperate Dan', a character from 'The Dandy' comic. The song finishes abruptly with a reprise of the 7/4 time signature melody sequence. Three songs in and the spirit of the 'classic' line-up of UFO is burning brightly.

'Stopped By A Bullet (Of Love)' (Schenker/Mogg)

As with 'Venus', 'Stopped...' opens with a blended acoustic and electric guitar riff, this time with a funk feel leading into a driving pop-rock story in familiar Mogg territory. Set in a remote bar in the Arizona desert, the tale is similar to 'Cherry'. The narrator meets an actress who 'thought I was in a band'. She becomes 'a pinball rolling round my head ... I found love for the very first time'.

Keyboards feature clearly in the mix as the chorus leads into Schenker's brief, growling solo. Post-solo, the narrator then meets 'Little Joe, is that your working name?' with another memorable couplet, 'Are you hiding something, or is the truth a darker stain?' A final chorus leads into a stunning, gorgeously toned guitar solo before the song ends in staccato fashion.

'Stopped...' is, however, the first non-essential track on *Walk On Water* and, after the classy heaviness which has preceded it, its poppy, acoustic-led instrumentation is at odds with the rest of the album.

'Darker Days' (Schenker/Mogg)

'Darker Days' has a hint of 'Mother Mary' about it with a magnificent heavy opening riff and mid-speed tempo, combined with Schenker's screaming lead interjections. Mogg's refrain at 0.31, 'I don't care what it's all about, I don't need to know', is superb, and at 1.12 a secondary, doom-laden riff enters and leads into the chorus, 'Darker days surround me now I'm older ... so help me please'.

After the second verse and chorus, there is a bridge section before Schenker's solo leads back into a reprise of the first verse. Mogg doesn't need to do this; as a skilled lyricist, he really should have come up with new words at this point rather than favour the disappointing cop-out of a straight repeat. Schenker again soars in the long fade out. 'Darker Days' is another entry in the 'hidden gem' category of UFO songs, taut, aggressive and melodic; it's the band doing what they do *so* well.

'Running On Empty' (Schenker/Mogg)
An energetic acoustic guitar introduction leads into another funky rhythm with the lyrics themed around a determination not to settle for the comforts of middle age, although the line 'I don't want Disney, I want to rock all night' is just terrible. The solo sections between the verses are a bit 'Guitar God By Numbers' and then the song moves into its bridge section, beginning 'No more pretty words...'.

So far so relatively so-so, until the surprising acoustic solo at 2.58 which is full of melody and overlaid guitars, before a return to a reprise of the first verse, which is, again, a missed opportunity. Schenker solos out over the fade and the overall feel of the song is one of worthy disposability. 'Running On Empty' is similar to 'Stopped...'; it feels like a step down from what the band are capable of, and have so amply demonstrated.

'Knock Knock' (Way/Mogg)
This straight forward heads-down rocker is Way's sole writing contribution. 'Knock Knock' dispenses with any dynamics and instead grooves along at a tempo that, like 'Pushed to The Limit' before it, could have done with more energy.

We are back in 'unhappy marriage/bitter divorce' territory although there are memorable lines including 'I'm not living anymore, I'm just breathing day to day' and 'Heaven's door has opened ... and there is no Mount Olympus just before you die'. The chorus has a sing-a-long refrain to it, and the bridge section is similarly bleak lyrically, although the overall musical feel is upbeat and celebratory. The final verse is the best, 'At the final curtain call, in the neon light display, I see all the ugly scars that illuminate my day'.

'Knock Knock' is an enjoyable romp of a track underneath Mogg's cynical words, where he may be commenting on the oft-married Way's approach to long-term relationships. The track ends with a favourite trick the band would frequently deploy live, the song finishing on a chord which is not the key chord that has dominated the rest of the number.

'Dreaming Of Summer' (Schenker/Mogg)
This song evokes past glories of 'Love To Love' with its elliptical, arpeggiated guitar ostinato, monumental power chords, drum fills, chugging semi-quaver rhythm, and lead guitar introduction.

The words are a real-world depiction of a man struggling against poor employment and financial prospects with a sense of resolve; 'When it comes right down to it, I've got to struggle through it'. The relentless rhythm relaxes into a half-tempo more reflective section (1.31) ('Put the lights way down low, come closer, tell me heroes don't fade away, they're forever'), Mogg's restrained vocal delivery lending an air of a ballad to this closing epic.

At 3.40 Schenker plays one of his simple, slow melodic lines to lead into the chorus which oddly only appears at this single point in the seven-minute-long song; 'I'm dreaming of summer, of just me and you now' which is interspersed with some gorgeously fluid bluesy guitar fills. At 4.49 a short, pretty acoustic guitar melody is heard, the introduction makes a truncated reappearance and this leads into the closing verses, Mogg's final lines are a reprise of his opening words which, on this occasion, work well: 'Woke up on a Manchester morning, no sun up in the sky, caught the train down to London, so broke it could make you cry'.

Schenker provides atmospheric fills as the song fades into the distance over the tonic chord chugging rhythm. Lyrically realistic and musically satisfying, 'Dreaming Of Summer' showcases the more balladic side of UFO to great effect and, but for the two self-cover songs, would have made a fine album closer.

Covenant

Personnel:
Phil Mogg: vocals
Michael Schenker: guitars
Pete Way: bass
Aynsley Dunbar: drums
Guest musicians:
Jesse Bradman and Luis Maldonado: backing vocals
Kevin Carlson: keyboards
Recorded at Prairie Sun Studios and LCM Studios, California.
Produced by UFO and Mike Varney
Released on the Steamhammer label: July 2000
Highest chart places: Did not chart

The tour to promote *Walk On Water* and the reformed 'classic' line-up featured Simon Wright, formerly of AC/DC and Dio, on drums. Andy Parker, fearing there would be problems with Schenker, decided to leave the band. Sure enough, after a series of incidents which resulted in the cancellation of gigs in the USA, Canada, and Germany, the mercurial guitarist quit UFO again during the autumn of 1995.

Due to the contractual conditions imposed by Schenker prior to *Walk On Water*, Mogg and Way reinvented themselves as 'Mogg/Way' and teamed up with guitarist George Belas and drummer Aynsley Dunbar to release *Edge Of The World* in June 1997 via Shrapnel Records. This album has some excellent rockers including 'Gravy Train', 'Fortune Town', 'History of Flames', and a stunning power-ballad in 'Saving Me From Myself'. Perversely there was another unnecessary self-cover, this time the victim was 'Mother Mary'.

Unfortunately, the project is let down by Belas's hard-edged, abrasive guitar tone, and his tendency to overplay *everything*. He suffers from an incurable case of 'Shredders Syndrome' with many of the album's songs overwhelmed by his incredibly fast runs to the detriment of the underlying music. The fact that Belas appears only as a single paragraph in this UFO history speaks volumes. The second, and final, 'Mogg/Way' album would feature a far more suitable guitarist.

Schenker reappeared on the UFO scene in 1997 and touring in Europe and the UK continued into early 1998. However, the German, never seemingly free of his demons, took flight once more during a Japanese tour which also led to Raymond's third departure from the band. UFO was once again laid to rest.

Whilst attempting a further reconciliation with Schenker, 'Mogg/Way' released *Chocolate Box* in September 1999, also on Shrapnel Records. This is the album which should have followed *Walk On Water,* being far closer to the 'classic' UFO sound. This time the pair were joined by Jeff Kolman on guitar, Paul Raymond, and Simon Wright.

Kolman is a far tastier player than Belas and is much more suited to the band's core sound. At times his tone is 'Schenker-esque', especially in his controlled use of wah-wah, but he is nobody's impressionist. His solos are melodic, full of feeling, and totally in keeping with the album's ten excellent songs. The overall tone and feel is less brutal than *Edge Of The World*, and the album is strong, classy and varied in style. Stand out tracks include 'Muddy's Gold', 'Jerusalem' and 'King Of The City', but pick any and disappointment is unlikely.

In 2000 Schenker rejoined UFO yet again and writing and recording of a new album commenced. When *Covenant* was released the critical consensus was that, whilst being excellent in patches, it didn't reach the high (walk-on) watermark of its now five-year-old predecessor. On the plus side, there are some very good, well-produced songs with their musical feet firmly planted in the familiar UFO terrain of power, melody and variety. On the minus side there just aren't enough of them.

A 'bonus' disc consisting of relatively recent tour material, *Live USA,* was included as part of the package. Recorded in 1998 straight from the mixing desk it featured Raymond and Wright alongside Schenker, Mogg and Way playing:
'Mother Mary', 'This Kid's', 'Let It Roll', 'Out In The Street', 'Venus', 'Pushed To The Limit', 'Love To Love'.

The CD booklet of *Covenant* is another disappointing oddity with an image of a typical 1950s B-movie-style UFO superimposed over a vast crowd of middle-aged men. It's all very grey and soul-destroying. A picture of the four band members is on the rear of the CD case with individual photos and pertinent information on the inside, although the lyrics are not included. Fortunately, the music is much better than the visuals

Covenant isn't as dull as its title or cover suggest. The album has a darker, more muscular mix than *Walk On Water* with the emphasis on clarity and heaviness. Acoustic guitar hardly features, and its absence adds to the increased power of the production. Keyboards support the songs from the background and there are some excellent backing vocals. Schenker's tone is exceptional and his playing is sometimes breathtaking, Mogg's vocals and lyrics are strong, whilst Way's contribution is largely restricted to bass duties. Dunbar is a highly effective rock drummer and fits right into the now officially four-piece line-up.

'Love Is Forever' (Schenker/Mogg)
Opening with bright, jangly, atonal arpeggios a heavy chord sequence sets up a strong groove with Mogg's vocals occasionally moving into falsetto. His possibly autobiographical lyrics, 'Rebel nature just got to be free' deal obliquely with a man torn between being in or out of a long term relationship, with occasional idiosyncratic references to 'flat caps and whippets'.

The chorus is softer, more reflectively melodic, and fuses effective keyboard support with tasteful fills from Schenker, as the female's perspective is taken,

'And she said, love is forever ... a slave for a fool'. The final sustained 'Love is...' of the second chorus blends Mogg's deepened, mature voice with the start of Schenker's fast and tuneful solo. There is a return to the bridge, and further choruses, followed by a fade of this unspectacular yet still reasonably satisfying opener.

'Unravelled' (Way/Mogg)
Way's basic, insistent riff combined with a relentless tribal drum rhythm underpins this tale of marital breakdown, the 'life of a cross-cut soul'. 'Unravelled' is heavier than 'Love Is Forever', musically less complex, and lyrically less subtle, 'When the honeymoon is over, she will suck out your brain'. The bridge section after the second chorus contains the memorable lines 'Great expectations will have a glitch, but a surge in the power may kill the bitch'. Schenker's solo matches the average quality of this unexceptional number with another brief solo over the fade. It's not exactly vintage UFO.

'Miss The Lights' (Schenker/Mogg)
Fortunately 'Miss The Lights' is the first of a trio of gems. A punchy rhythmic chord sequence with a simple guitar melody which will become the chord progression for the chorus leads into this mid-paced vehicle for Mogg's sardonic lyrics, 'Walk in tall, full of tedious charm ... don't you know who I am?'.

In the chorus his deprecating, short laughs may be as intentionally self-mocking as the lines 'Guess you miss the lights, I guess you miss the fame, I guess you miss everybody, hanging onto your name'. After the second chorus, there is a half-tempo sequence ('Sometimes when you're all alone and the blue turns to grey, better get down on those pinkie knees, and start to pray'), before another chorus which leads into Schenker's adequate solo, with keyboard support.

The half tempo section returns briefly as part of the instrumental, before the third verse and repeated choruses lead into a fade with Schenker soloing against Mogg's falsetto 'Whoo-hoos' and isolated lines from the chorus. The downside of the song is its underpowered tempo, but it's a step up from how *Covenant* commenced.

'Midnight Train' (Schenker/Mogg)
This riotous stormer should have been the opening track. Full of energy and drive, it's archetypal UFO and featured briefly in the live set of the period. The excellent chorus, 'Come out of the rain, come out of the night, riding the midnight train', is again supported by excellent backing vocals and subtle keyboards.

A half-tempo instrumental features a superb sounding, highly melodic Schenker lead line, before dropping into a lower register riff in 6/4 time. This then goes up through the gears to the original speed, and another excellent flying solo leads back into the opening riff with an overlaid slide guitar melody.

A final, shortened verse and more choruses move into a fade with the guitarist again letting loose. 'Midnight Train' is another magnificent example of UFO at their best, the Schenker/Mogg alchemy producing more musical gold.

'Fool's Gold' (Schenker/Mogg)
'Fool's Gold' is really two songs in one, neither bearing any relation to the other. The first is a beautiful short ballad with shades of 'Belladonna' about it. Mogg's soulful contribution is superb, 'Fool's gold, sparkling like the midnight sun, fool's gold, touch the ivory handles on my gun', being particularly evocative. Way's bass and the subdued keyboards add much to the emotive atmosphere.

At 1.31 the second song kicks in at a furious tempo, with Dunbar's double bass drums powering the band along. Featuring a particularly fiddly Schenker riff Mogg unleashes more memorable lyrics, 'Sometimes, in the dark, when hope is fading, all the long goodbyes, want to sympathise, spend my time getting high'. The chorus is positive and uplifting: 'Someone came to rescue me … someone came to take me home'. By now the track is fantastically powerful and it's a joy to hear the band firing on all cylinders.

The chorus leads into another section of twisty guitar motifs moving between 4/4 and 7/4 time, and another highly impressive solo rises up to lead into further choruses which then fade quickly with another fiery fretboard display. 'Fool's Gold' is the standout track on *Covenant* and sounds fresh, exciting and original, proof if it were needed that the magic was still there, even if it wasn't consistently present.

'In The Middle Of Madness' (Schenker/Mogg)
Starting with a poppy, distorted guitar riff this up-tempo major key groover could have been a single, with its strong commercial melodies and straightforward verse/chorus structure. Lyrically Mogg describes the first intoxicating feeling of being in love, 'In the middle of madness, she walks, she breathes Babylon'. The solo section is relatively straightforward, Schenker emphasising melody over flashy pyrotechnics, and the entire song is reminiscent of Cheap Trick's style of power pop-rock commerciality. That's not in any way a bad thing – it's just not a UFO thing.

'The Smell Of Money' (Schenker/Mogg)
'The Smell Of Money' opens with a guitar solo over downward crashing power chords, before falling into a complex riff in 15/16 time. The song moves into 4/4 time for the verses where the subject matter could be an update of the protagonist from 'Lettin' Go', twenty-five years on, 'One more day, with a terminal fall … it's an open coffin, needs one more nail'.

Another half-tempo, quieter section breaks up the firepower with swirling keyboards and backing vocals. After a repeat of the verse/bridge structure there is a reprise of the introduction which leads into another dreamlike passage, 'Stretched out across the ceiling, prayer domes shimmer and glow, golden citadels, while the awning billows and flows'. A classic Schenker mid-range melody, slow and simple, is followed by a return to the chorus riff over which he solos. Another verse and chorus with prominent keyboards lead to a sudden, stabbed end.

'Rise Again' (Way/Mogg)
Way's opening bass melody, evoking memories of 'Cherry', is underpinned by soft keyboards and guitar with Mogg's mature voice describing an idyllic scene, 'Going to Jamaica, warm and coral waters flow, there she goes, sun kissed her body, in this magic, feel love grow'. The dynamics shift dramatically for 'Feel like letting go' as the song moves into a heady, heavy, slow blues riff, the keyboards adding real weight to the music.

The vocals are exceptional here, sung with real passion and fire, 'With a great escape, I'll be there ... I'm gonna stand up, gonna rise again'. Schenker employs a less overdriven sound for his solo which features harmonised phrases towards its end. The song ends as it started, with subtlety ('Dreamtime Devinia, feel like letting go'). 'Rise Again' is a gem, full of power, melody and dynamics, it's up there with the best songs on the album.

'Serenade' (Schenker/Mogg)
The opening minute of 'Serenade' could qualify as an entry for 'Eurovision'. The song is based around a strummed chord sequence rather than a definitive guitar riff, and a singsong guitar melody. While lyrically it's ordinary, the mixture of guitars, backing vocals and keyboards keep it from moving too far towards 'Cheese-Central'.

At 1.18 there is an unexpected heavy guitar melody section before a return to the memorable opening guitar melody. The bridge section beginning 'Out on the beach is a footprint of the soul', leads into another excellent guitar section, followed by a surprise as the main body of the instrumental is played on acoustic guitar. Mogg returns with a disappointing repeat of the first verse, and Schenker adds his opening refrain which moves up a key as he overlays his initial melody with an unnecessary additional solo to a fade. It sounds too busy and detracts from the melodic quality of what has preceded it.

'Cowboy Joe' (Schenker/Mogg)
Another heavy 15/16 time riff opens this mid-tempo chord-based driving track which has a 'metal country' feel to the chorus. After the bridge, the song takes an unexpected sharp turn into a half-tempo quieter solo section. This mixes Hawaiian style slide guitar and gently picked clean electric lines with effective support from the bass and keyboards.

The initial riff then returns with a short, furiously fast run and the main solo over the verse chord sequence. Following another verse, there are further choruses leading to the fade-out. Despite the mid-song instrumental invention 'Cowboy Joe' comes across as an inessential track, disposable and forgettable.

'The World And His Dog' (Schenker/Mogg)

Finally, some genuine heavy melodic rock passion returns with a fast triplet riff and powerful drum rhythms leading into a heavy descending chord sequence. Mogg unleashes his best lyrics of the album, '... the bodies are buried, freeways and wells, boneyards with vistas, gateways to hell', before rising to the chorus, 'When it's all over, you're brown bread....', a peculiarly English phrase which would confuse listeners unfamiliar with Cockney rhyming slang. The second verse contains more poetic lines, 'Out looking for Venus, she's black marble on ice, cut to precision, weighted like dice'.

After the second chorus, Schenker's solo is a spectacular display of speed before relaxing into a more controlled set of phrases over the verse chord sequence. At 2.23 the mood changes again with an irregular time signature and syncopation, together with a growling mid-range guitar melody, before returning to repeats of the chorus, 'Maybe you'll make it, maybe you won't, the world and his dog, won't care if you don't'. The song finishes with the initial aggressive riff leading to a sudden stop.

'The World and His Dog' is another gem, packed with energy, power, and melody, and is a fine final track. If *Covenant* had more songs like this, it would easily have been the equal of *Walk On Water* and, given its heavier, darker production, could even have bettered it.

Sharks

Personnel:
Phil Mogg: vocals
Michael Schenker: guitars
Pete Way: bass
Aynsley Dunbar: drums
Guest musicians:
Jesse Bradman, Luis Maldonado: backing vocals
Kevin Carlson: keyboards
Mike Varney: guitar
Recorded at Prairie Sun Studios, California
Produced by Mike Varney and Steve Fontano
Released on the Steamhammer label: September 2002
Highest chart places: Did not chart

The *Covenant* tour saw yet another UFO line-up with Luis Maldonado on
rhythm guitar and keyboards, and Jeff Martin on drums. With a sense of
inevitability the band crashed yet again, this time near the end of a UK tour in
Manchester in November 2000, Schenker again being the culprit.

In 2002 Mogg released his first solo album *Dancing With St. Peter* under the
band name '$ign of 4', (the title of a 'Sherlock Holmes' novel by Sir Arthur
Conan-Doyle). Featuring Jeff Kolman (guitars), Jimmy Curtain (bass), Shane
Gaalaas (drums), and Mark Renk (keyboards) it's a sublime piece of work.
The songs ooze melody, class and power throughout. Kolman's playing is
exceptional and tasteful in equal measure, and Mogg soars both lyrically and
vocally. Whilst the standout song is the title track ballad, there is plenty of
high quality, melodic, hard rock on offer including 'Overload', 'Driven' and
'Song Keeps A Coming'. *Dancing With St. Peter* should have paved the way
for Kolman as a 'shoo-in' for the increasingly erratic Schenker, the American's
playing and writing skills being the perfect foil for the latter-day Mogg's talents.
This could have been the future…

However, Schenker, Way and Mogg re-assembled UFO for what would be
their final album together. If *Walk On Water* strode confidently across the
surface, and *Covenant* spent some time submerged, *Sharks* is floundering
around in the depths, drowning not waving. The underwhelming front cover
is a close-up image of, inventively, a shark, while the back cover has a group
photo of the four-man line-up. Mogg, Dunbar and Way look suitably moody
and rock-ready. Schenker's appearance answers the question 'What do you
get if you cross a hipster with a yeti?' The deterioration in the guitarist's look
is sadly matched by his creativity and contribution to this project. On the
inner pages of the CD booklet, the song's lyrics are reproduced, sometimes
inaccurately, with individual pictures of the band amidst the usual information.

The most disappointing feature of *Sharks* is Schenker's playing. For much
of the album, it sounds as if his mind is elsewhere as he rehashes phrases and

ideas from the past. He has also altered his familiar guitar tone to something less overdriven for his solos and even on the odd occasion when it is cranked up, he sounds neither inspired nor inspiring. Also underperforming is the usual creative chemistry between guitarist and lyricist which this time fails to produce much in the way of really good material. There is barely anything here to match the better tracks on *Covenant* and it doesn't come close to touching *Walk On Water*. The reformed band peaked straight away with *Walk On Water* and from that point on the trajectory was sadly downwards. This is the mirror opposite of the band's progression from *Phenomenon* to *Strangers*.

For his part Mogg has either been reading a lot of history or is suffering from a severe case of nostalgia, as several songs have references to people and events from the past. *Sharks* does have the occasional flickering of former greatness, but nothing here has really stood the test of time, and some of the tracks are just dreadful, unworthy of the band's name.

There was no supporting tour for *Sharks*. It seemed an ignoble end to what had promised so much when *Walk On Water* had appeared. Again, health issues, personality clashes, and chemical dependencies served yet again to undermine a fine legacy and bring a halt to a second 'Golden Age' which had always promised more than it had delivered.

'Outlaw Man' (Mogg/Way)
Opening with an impressive slide guitar riff, 'Outlaw Man' soon descends into the tired, dreary trudge of a too-slow chugger. The first of Mogg's nostalgia lyrics has references to the 1950s (when 'men were men'), The Red Rooster, Elvis and Steve McQueen. The chorus, 'I'm a rocker ... I am one big bone...' is dire, and the bridge section, 'I'm one of life's miracles...' shows little improvement.

There's a reprise of the introduction leading into Schenker's underpowered solo which is slightly lifted by a brief melodic pattern at 2.14 with the wah-wah pedal much in evidence. But then we're back into the verse, chorus and repeated bridge structure until the track ends as it began. When the best parts of a track are the first and last fifteen seconds it really doesn't bode well for the next ten songs.

'Quicksilver Rider' (Schenker/Mogg)
Quicksilver is the name of a dragon created by fantasy writer Michael Kornarck. Whether Mogg is a fan of this genre of fiction is not known but the time-travelling nature of his lyrics does suggest a possible link.

The fast-paced introduction bears a resemblance to Rush's 'The Analog Kid', from their 1982 album *Signals*. 'Quicksilver Rider' then moves into a clean guitar-driven funky riff underpinned by a pulsating semiquaver rhythm. Mogg's first verse serves up the San Francisco Gold Rush, which leads into an excellent section with references to Attila (The Hun), Genghis Khan, Napoleon, and Nelson. The chorus has an epic quality to its arrangement with plenty of melody, but then it's back to the history lesson, this time featuring Moses, Jezebel, and partying with Nero 'as Rome burned and fell'.

Schenker's solo has a bewildering country music feel to it before moving onto meatier sounds for its conclusion. The final section of the story deals with the nuclear bomb dropped towards the end of the Second World War and, paradoxically, praying with Gandhi. The chorus is repeated twice with the song coming to a sudden stop after a repeat of the introduction. 'Quicksilver Rider' is an improvement, but not a huge one.

'Serenity' (Schenker/Mogg)
In the inner pages of the accompanying CD booklet the words 'Do What!' are added in brackets to the title, but they don't appear elsewhere or in the song itself.

'Serenity' opens with a subdued chorus with just vocals, quiet guitar, and subtle counter-pointed bass. Then a fantastic, slow-burning, heavy chord based riff is unleashed, the additional instrumentation bringing to mind 'Stargazer' from Rainbow's 1976 album *Rising*. The pre-chorus, ('And it goes around, round and round again'), leads into a melodic and heavily textured chorus with choral style backing vocals filling all available spaces. Mogg's lyrics have more relevance and bite than anything Ronnie James Dio could come up with, 'Out from the marble palaces, Kings and Queens will rejoice, their importance of being, their importance of choice' whilst 'The Pope blessed his children, in a sea of sleaze'.

After the chorus, there is an instrumental over a new chord sequence, followed by a memorable low register melody from Schenker who then launches into a heavily wah-wah'd solo which is a long way from his best work. It sounds as if he deemed his fret-board doodles to be good enough for the final take, and no-one suggested otherwise. As anticipated, there is another verse, pre-chorus and further choruses to end with, and another wandering solo to the fade. 'Serenity' has an epic quality to it which is let down, as are so many songs on *Sharks,* by the guitarist's mostly lacklustre efforts.

'Deadman Walking' (Schenker/Mogg)
A clean 'Shadows'-like guitar melody sits on top of a steady driving rhythm in this light pop-rock-style song. Some crunchy guitar chords add some much-needed heft to the texture. After the first verse, the music drops into a different chord sequence with some indistinct dialogue which may be from a film or television programme, but cannot be identified clearly.

A tuneful chorus arrives to lift the mood with effective backing vocals, and Schenker provides another short, underpowered instrumental interlude before moving into a fierier solo over the verse chord structure. There is a return to the interlude and then the song is into its final third with all the expected ingredients. Schenker solos in sadly predictable fashion over the fade, and 'Deadman Walking' has become another disposable number which lacks any real inspiration or interest.

'Shadow Dancer' (Schenker/Mogg/ Fontano)

The start of the opening riff, which is similar to 'Darker Days', is quickly interspersed with some cleaner picked descending arpeggio patterns before an organ sound joins the mix leading into the verse. Mogg seems to be basing his delivery on Aerosmith's Steven Tyler, his vocals having a similar funky feel to 'Walk This Way'.

The pre-chorus loses this influence and the actual chorus is similarly superior with its sing-a-long 'Back on my wall, shadow dancer' refrain. Schenker's solo again disappoints and Mogg similarly seems to have lost his muse with the lines 'I'm lucky in life, unlucky in love, no special blessing from above'. The rest of the song unfolds exactly as you would expect it to.

'Someone's Gonna Have To Pay' (Mogg/Way)

Not only the worst song on the album but, excluding most of *UFO1* and all but one track from *Flying*, the worst song the band had recorded to date. It starts with a tired retread of the 'Doctor Doctor' shuffle rhythm and then works its long way inexorably downwards to life-sappingly tedious. There is an initially promising chord-based guitar riff followed by another dull little solo with its roots again in country and blues.

Mogg's delivery initially sounds either lazy or drunk depending upon your mood, and there are more nostalgic references: 'Moon-shots, rockets, 1960s cool, Sonny Boy Williamson, Pope John Paul, the Congo and the Vietnam, the Beatles to the Stones' before finally arriving at the point of his words: 'There's nobody left gonna shake these bones'. The chorus is catchy and has some character about it, but the repeated refrains of 'someone's gonna have to pay' quickly become tiresome.

If you are feeling charitable Schenker's solo sounds like he was experimenting with guitar sounds in the studio before the 'recording' light came on. If you're not, it's a dog's dinner. Then there is a curious spoken word sequence from Mogg leading into another verse, and there's still over two *long* minutes to go. Another solo section has Schenker wandering around the fretboard in a bewildered haze with plenty of wah-wah abuse and very little else.

All good things come to an end and, eventually, so too does this embarrassment with an abrupt stop. This song should never have made the final cut, and whilst its omission wouldn't have saved *Sharks* at least it wouldn't have dragged it down quite so far. 'Someone's Gonna Have To Pay' is that rare example of a song achieving sentience and deciding to bore itself to death.

'Sea Of Faith' (Schenker/Mogg/Fontano)

'Sea Of Faith' has a similar 'Eurovision' opening feel to 'Serenade', with a simple strummed chord sequence leading into a sub-funk rhythm supported by some well-placed keyboards. The verse is routine, but the pre-chorus, 'Cover me in roses, put nickels on my eyes,' is better leading into a strong chorus, 'Sea of faith ... I'm just here to watch the river flow'.

Schenker solos over a new chord progression but again it's nothing special. At 3.17 there is a brief and unexpected turn into a subtle arpeggio sequence with a quiet guitar melody and some short, savage distorted interjections, then it's time for the last verse, which just repeats the first verse.

The coda section contains, finally, a memorable guitar melody which fades too quickly. 'Sea Of Faith' is another highly melodic rock song which would have sat well on *Covenant,* but here it shows up the paucity of most of the other *Sharks* songs only too sharply.

'Fighting Man' (Mogg/Way)
'Fighting Man' is your archetypal, Way-riffed, crowd-pleasing rocker. It's UFO-by-numbers, simple in structure, mid-paced in tempo, and foot-tappingly effective. Schenker manages to pull off a reasonable solo prior to the bridge section, ('ashes to ashes ... trash is still trash'), and like 'Sea Of Faith' it's a good song *for this album.*

Surprisingly, producer Mike Varney plays the lead guitar fills towards the end of the track (3.47), and his playing is no better or worse than Schenker's at this point, which says something. Unexpectedly 'Fighting Man' would appear in the early set-lists of the Vinnie Moore era. Whilst being decent enough in an unspectacular way it's not exactly top-drawer material.

'Perfect View' (Schenker/Mogg/Fontano)
This is the last halfway decent UFO song to feature Schenker. Opening with a driving riff over which the rhythm kicks in and the verse begins, the song explodes gloriously 30 seconds in with 'And she mesmerises, captivates, a message for a heart that aches' and some superb accompanying guitar work.

The chorus chord sequence brings back memories of 'Doing It All for You'. Words-wise Mogg is below par, an example from the third verse being '21 is easy, but I don't know why, there's no difference, this bird will fly' which reads more like a complex crossword clue than a rock song lyric.

Schenker goes foraging around in his bag of clichés to piece together a brisk solo which sounds like he heard the underlying chord structure for the first time only a few minutes previously. Again Mogg resorts to repeating the first verse as the last verse, and the final choruses lead into further dull guitar fills as the track fades away.

'Crossing Over' (Schenker/Mogg)
Starting with a heavy chord sequence, this medium slow-paced misery is a band running (on) empty of inspiration. The verse is tired, the chorus dire, and the bridge section sounds like it was written because most songs have a bridge section. Every component in this stodgy disappointment sounds bored and wishes it was somewhere, anywhere else.

The instrumental section features a strange melodic progression which passes through unusual chord changes but is of passing interest only because what surrounds it is so downright disappointing. The sound of the wah-wah pedal announces the final Schenker solo which is cut off in its lack of prime by a return to the opening sequence. And the song just drones on with more inconsequential contributions from Mogg before the final choruses which repeat and fade with the inevitable guitar fills.

'Hawaii' (Schenker)

Pointless. This brief instrumental features two clean sounding guitars, one strumming chords, the other a slide-based 'melody' of Schenker playing with himself. For a man who is revered by some as a 'Guitar God', this truly is a piece which passeth all understanding.

You Are Here

Personnel:
Phil Mogg: vocals
Vinnie Moore: guitars
Paul Raymond: keyboards
Pete Way: bass
Jason Bonham: drums and backing vocals
Recorded at Area 51 Studios, Celle, Germany
Produced, recorded and engineered by Tommy Newton.
Released on the Steamhammer label: March 2004
Highest chart places: Did not chart

In January 2003 it was announced that Schenker had left UFO. This was the German's fifth and final exit and, given the disappointment of *Sharks* and the guitarist's history of unreliable behaviour, non-appearances, and onstage meltdowns, nobody was surprised

In September 2003 a four-disc live box set *Live On Earth* was issued via Zoom Club. This featured concerts in Vienna (January 1998), Cleveland (July 1977) and Cincinatti (August 1995). For the discs recorded in 1995 and 1998, the line up was Mogg, Schenker, Way, Raymond, and Wright. The 1977 disc naturally featured Andy Parker on drums.

Discs One and Two (Vienna)

'Natural Thing', 'Mother Mary', 'A Self Made Man', 'Electric Phase', 'This Kid's', 'Out In The Street', 'One More For The Rodeo', 'Venus', 'Pushed To The Limit', 'Love To Love', 'Too Hot To Handle', 'Only You Can Rock Me', 'Lights Out', 'Doctor, Doctor', 'Rock Bottom', 'Shoot Shoot'

Disc Three (Cleveland)

'Lights Out', 'Getting' Ready', 'Love To Love', 'On With The Action', 'Doctor Doctor', 'Out In The Streets', 'This Kid's', 'Shoot Shoot', 'Rock Bottom', 'Too Hot To Handle'

Disc Four (Cincinnati)

'Natural Thing', 'Mother Mary', 'Let It Roll', 'This Kid's', 'Out In The Street', 'Venus', 'Pushed To The Limit', 'Love To Love', 'Only You Can Rock Me', 'Too Hot To Handle', 'Lights Out', 'Doctor, Doctor', 'Rock Bottom', 'Shoot Shoot', 'C'mon Everybody'

The Vienna discs sound excellent, the Cleveland and Cincinnati recordings are, sadly, poor quality bootleg rough.

On the hunt for the band's eighth lead guitarist, Mogg made overtures to John Norum of Europe, who declined. The position was finally taken by Vinnie Moore, one of the darlings of the Eighties shredder scene, and this signalled the beginning of a relatively settled line-up. Moore would go on to become the band's longest-serving guitarist, playing on six consecutive studio albums.

Was Moore the best choice as UFO's new fret burner? Mogg clearly thought so, although both Laurence Archer and, especially, Jeff Kolman had justifiable claims to the position. Fans who hoped for a return of Paul Chapman to the fold were also to be disappointed. Paul Raymond rejoined for his fourth sojourn, and the drum stool was occupied by Jason Bonham whose father, John, had had some degree of success with another English rock band during the 1970s.

The onerous 'Schenker Conditions' were dispensed with by a simple phone call between the two protagonists. Mogg asked for the rights to the band's name back and Schenker acquiesced. UFO could now take flight without him, and they took full advantage of the opportunity. Three-fifths of the 'classic' line-up combined with two new, highly experienced and talented musicians would push the latest version of UFO to impressive levels of confidence and songwriting quality.

You Are Here is an album of superior, melodic hard rock, and both it and the subsequent tour went a long way to restoring the band's reputation. Infinitely better than *Sharks*, *You Are Here* shows them almost back to their best and joins *Walk On Water, The Wild...*, and *Obsession* as peaks of their recording career.

By playing shred less and the song more, together with his substantial songwriting contribution, Moore's appointment is fully justified. Mogg's lyrical and vocal performances are amongst his finest work, whilst Bonham is a real find adding, unsurprisingly, more than a hint of Zeppelin-esque power with his pile-driving drumming, together with a distinctively throaty style of backing vocal.

The unusual cover artwork is also a distinct improvement on the three previous releases. It features the long shadow of a man standing diagonally across an arid, sunny landscape, whilst the rear has a woman's shadow in the same position. The CD booklet contains the song lyrics and a black and white group photo. The Japanese release included an extra track, 'Messing Up The Bed', which is a slow-burning, heavy blues number concerning the disintegration of a relationship, with a sing-a-long chorus and plenty of lead guitar.

'When Daylight Goes To Town' (Moore/Mogg)
The opening shot of the new era begins with a strident chord-based riff, joined by a melodic guitar line and organ as the song moves into an AC/DC style loping rhythm. Mogg is in fine, mature voice in this confident mid-tempo foot-tapper with excellent lines including 'Sometimes I wake and I think of you, forgetting that you're dead' and 'I still have your photograph, picks me up when I'm feeling down'. Moore introduces effective slide guitar which leads into the chorus, and his first solo is excellent with little evidence of his shredding reputation.

A quieter version of the opening riff with harmonised guitar fills follows, together with a clap-a-long, four-to-the-floor bass drum beat. This moves into the final verse, and further choruses with more guitar fills before the song comes to a sudden harmonised stop.

'When Daylight Goes To Town' is a solid, reassuring opener and indicative of the quality that is to come. In just one song the band demonstrates just how far they have moved on from the sorry mess that was *Sharks*.

'Black Cold Coffee' (Moore/Mogg)

'Black Cold Coffee' is even better. A galloping drum introduction leads into a fast, complex, syncopated riff and Mogg's obscurely worded tale of 'Captain Midnight and Captain Cruise' The song moves up a gear with the superb 'Out in the madness somewhere in Orleans' section leading into a raucous chorus. This new UFO sounds alive and vital, brimming with energy and confidence. Moore's rhythm guitar is aggressively chunky in the second verse, and Mogg is particularly on point with the lines 'They travelled up together from the coast, east of Aldgate, silently like ghosts'.

After the second chorus, another excellent riff sets Moore in motion for his solo which contains some Schenker-esque runs with hints of shred amidst the melody. There is a return to the final chorus with a repeated syncopated phrase which ends on a held chord. UFO's trademarks of power and melody are back at full strength and these new songs are breaths of very welcome fresh air.

'The Wild One' (Moore/Mogg)

The pace slows. Starting with an overdriven chord riff and an overlaid melody from Moore, Mogg supplies more opaque lyrics dealing with the remnants of a past relationship which ended badly. Slide guitar features in the build-up to the chorus, which is full of power, melody and expression. 'The Wild One' is the first song on the album to properly showcase the band's use of dynamics in the rise and fall of the music.

Moore's solo features some interesting rapid harmonised phrases together with a spectacularly pyrotechnic run towards its close. In the third verse, an acoustic guitar and counter-pointed bass underpin more memorable lyrics, 'Sometimes I stop breathing, just to feel reborn, it's like rolling thunder, blowing through the corn', which is followed by a further song-centric guitar solo.

The final section, 'And I'm out here drifting, a million miles from home, floating in a space ship or falling like a stone', increases the power which suddenly reverts to an acoustic guitar-led gentle ending, another fine example of the many facets of the band.

'Give It Up' (Moore/Way/Mogg)

Opening with a slow, heavy introduction with the vocals straight in from the start, 'Give It Up' then falls into a typical mid-tempo driving rocker. Mogg's vocal phrasing and tone are first class, and the bridge is similarly excellent. The chorus sits over the same chord progression as the verse, but here Moore overdoes it to the point where virtually every breath Mogg takes is filled with some short lead lines. The lyricist paraphrases Oscar Wilde in the second verse, 'I've laid down in the gutter, looking up at the stars', before adding his own downbeat lines 'Washed by the rain, and these passing cars'.

The guitar solo occurs over a new chord progression, and when Moore reduces the shredder facet of his technique, his playing is excellent. There is a reprise of the half-tempo chord introduction before repeated choruses with an additional solo as the song fades. 'Give It Up' is a slight step down from the quality of the preceding numbers, but this is small criticism given the high-quality level already established. It's still head and shoulders above just about everything on *Sharks*.

'Call Me' (Moore/Mogg)

Bonham's 'Son-of-Zeppelin' influence is plain for all to hear on this slower-paced, epic-sounding, heavy blues number. The lyrics are excellent from the start, for instance 'She looked for truth inside a bottle of rain, posted an ad then changed her name', as is the memorably melodic chorus, 'Call me, don't let me down, walk me on the water, don't let me drown' supported by Bonham's characteristic backing vocals. The second verse continues the lyrical quality, 'You don't need one more to shed one more tear'.

Moore's solo has a melancholy air to it, with long 'violined' notes over subtle keyboards, before the heaviness returns. Unfortunately, this is where he becomes overly reliant on open string trickiness and repeated rapid pull-offs at the expense of melody. The final choruses lead into a repeat of the opening riff, which ends abruptly.

'Slipping Away' (Moore/Mogg)

Suddenly there is an abrupt change of mood and style for the first ballad of the album. Opening with a pretty, arpeggiated guitar sequence, a slow riff is established over which Moore adds an effective acoustic guitar melody. Electric and acoustic guitars are blended into a hypnotic rhythm with harmony lines featuring in the memorable chorus, 'The closer you get, the further you slip away'.

There is a beautiful section at 2.49 featuring some quiet single notes treated with delay over a softly strummed acoustic rhythm as Mogg paints more vivid pictures, 'These plastic bags and crushed up cans, this twisted wreck on some foreign land, better hold close what you hold so dear, 'cos the vanishing point is coming oh so near'. Repeated chorus phrases with effective harmonised guitar fills lead into the song's coda, as it slows and ends on another held chord. Reassuringly, the quality of the ballads from the new line-up is just as strong as the rockers.

'The Spark That Is Us' (Moore/Mogg/Bonham/Raymond)

Another song that cannot deny its Zeppelin influence, 'The Spark That Is Us' has a slow, menacing groove which mixes three bars of 4/4 time and a single bar of 2/4 under the verse, before staying in 4/4 for Mogg's excellent bridge section, 'All the misfits are flying like a kite, all of my friends have come to see the fight'. The chorus is top-notch, packed with melody and emotion, with Bonham contributing muscular drums.

After another verse, bridge and chorus, Moore's excellent solo follows the initial riff with some short, harmonised phrases. The album's heaviest section arrives at 3.03 with a new dirty, funky guitar and bass riff, before further choruses lead to the song's fade. Whilst occasionally inviting the question 'What would UFO sound like if they covered Led Zeppelin songs?', this remains a compellingly strong track which plays to the band's strengths.

'Sympathy' (Raymond)

'Sympathy's evocative keyboard introduction initially brings back traumatic memories of *Misdemeanor*. Luckily this is short-lived as subtle guitar fills and spacious bass lines give way to more fine lyrics, 'So you've seen the sunrise on the Nile, solved the mystery of the Mona Lisa smile', with Moore's harmonised lines reminiscent of Brian May's work on the early Queen albums.

This subtle mood is destroyed by the heavy chorus, 'There ain't no sympathy at all ... I've got to find someone to make me happy'. A softer second verse follows with effective, sustained keyboard and guitar backing, before another chorus complete with bluesy fills. Moore's main solo is excellent, fast, and melodic, and a repeated section of choruses moves into the song's conclusion on another held chord. That's seven excellent tracks in a row...

'Mr Freeze' (Moore/Mogg)

The first of the album's two consecutive non-essential numbers, 'Mr Freeze' opens with a vaguely country-style overdriven guitar riff with Mogg in a reflective mood, 'This year I've been feeling kinda weary, next year I may not come back at all, sometimes I hear the angels singing, or I can hear my mother's call'. The slow tempo and ordinary chorus fleshed out with acoustic guitar, fail to maintain this song at the heights already scaled, although Mogg's memorable lines 'There's a touch of humour in everything I see, there's touch of scorn' are well phrased.

The instrumental section has a sparse feel, initially with subtle phrasings from Moore before an impressively heavy funk riff brings forth his innate shredderiness and a formulaic solo – lots of notes, all very impressive from a technical point of view, but un-involving emotionally. Further choruses lead to a reprise of the introduction and a slowed end.

'Jello Man' (Moore/Mogg)

'Jello Man' is similar funked-up filler. Its high point is the bridge section which is melodic and lyrically strong, 'All dressed up in the King's new clothes, climbing up the monkey's nose, standing out like a stiff on parade, you're overworked and you're underpaid'. The chorus, played over the opening riff, isn't great and outstays its welcome despite some interesting backwards-recorded vocals.

113

The solo is set against a laid back country-meets-funk setting before Moore unleashes the horses and goes for it. There follows another set of choruses and this unspectacular song comes to a close with a jerky, syncopated riff and a sudden stop.

'Baby Blue' (Moore/Mogg)

A tasteful acoustic guitar introduction, with subtle overlaid electric fills ushers in a classic of UFO's latest period. Fine lyrics are underpinned by classy, sustained keyboards, 'Bet you never thought, time would go so fast, bet you never thought a memory could last. Is it wrapped up in boxes, with your fashion crazes, packed all away with life's scars and grazes?' After an excellent chorus, electric guitar, bass and drums join and move the song into a heavier setting, before going into a muscular, melodic second verse where once again Mogg's words and singing are first class.

The bridge section recalls a lyrical theme of *Walk On Water*, age being no barrier to ambition, life not being over despite there being less years ahead than behind you. This leads into a repeat of the introduction, with Moore's beautiful solo played solely on acoustic guitar, against a restrained rhythmic backing. The relative heaviness returns, ('Going round and round and round in my little world'), before the coda with just Mogg, Moore and Way bringing this outstanding number to a soft conclusion.

'Swallow' (Moore/Bonham/Mogg)

You Are Here closes with a ballad. Opening with an understated electric guitar introduction, a slow groove rhythm is set in motion. Moving into an excellent bridge ('Out on this lonely road, cold coffee and a cigarette, making a long-distance call, on some losing bet'), the uplifting chorus becomes more intense with Bonham's strong-toned backing vocals.

After a second verse, bridge, and chorus Moore's solo is isolated with no other instruments playing, an unusual move and indicative of the confidence the band has in their new material. He is joined by drums and bass, and concludes with suitable shredding and impressive harmonised lines. The chorus is repeated to end the album on a final sustained tonic chord.

'Swallow' is an excellent final track and rounds off a collection which shows, as has been demonstrated amply in the past, that there is life, and lots of it, after Schenker.

The Monkey Puzzle

Personnel:
Phil Mogg: vocals
Vinnie Moore: guitars
Paul Raymond: keyboards, backing vocals
Pete Way: bass
Andy Parker: drums
Guest musicians:
Michael Roth: harmonica
Martina Frank, Kalle Bosel: backing vocals
Recorded at Area 51 Studios, Celle, Germany
Drums recorded at Big House Studios, Hanover, Germany
Guitars recorded at Vinman Studios, USA
Produced, recorded and engineered by Tommy Newton
Released on the Steamhammer label: September 2006
Highest chart places: Did not chart

Fresh from the positive reactions of both fans and critics to *You Are Here*, UFO toured extensively and released a double live CD *Showtime* in 2005. Recorded on 13 May 2005 in Wilhelmshaven, Germany, it featured powerful performances of:

'Mother Mary', 'When Daylight Goes To Town', 'Let It Roll', 'I'm A Loser', 'This Kid's', 'The Wild One', 'Fighting Man', 'Only You Can Rock Me', 'Baby Blue', 'Mr Freeze', 'Love To Love', 'Too Hot To Handle', Lights Out, 'Rock Bottom', 'Doctor Doctor', 'Shoot Shoot'

A companion two-DVD pack with the same title was also issued with the interesting bonus of the band playing some favourite fan songs in Peppermint Park Studios on 26 May 2005:
'Pack It Up And Go', 'Try Me', 'Love To Love', 'Slipping Away', 'Cherry', 'Profession Of Violence'

'Try Me', 'Love To Love' and 'Profession Of Violence' featured a string quartet (two violins, a viola and a cello,) as an interesting alternative to the synthesiser sound used in live performance.

Bonham, however, was becoming disillusioned with the UFO lifestyle due to their continuing copious substance abuse – mindful, no doubt, of his own father's premature death from similar excesses. Meanwhile, Andy Parker was considering a return to music. Contacted by Paul Raymond with news of the upcoming vacancy, Parker decided to throw his lot back in with his old friends and rejoined the band.

The CD's bemusing cover shows the interior of a completely white room with a single white armchair and a large flat-screen television which is broadcasting the image of a young man dressed in white with his back towards the viewer. On the rear of the booklet is a colour photo of the latest line-up taken inside what looks like a poly-tunnel. Mogg is crouching, the others are standing moodily behind him, and inside the booklet is another band photo with Mogg the only one in focus. Scattered throughout the lyric pages are individual pictures of the band.

The overall feel of *The Monkey Puzzle* is of the band taking its foot off the accelerator and coasting. There is some sterling work here, but equally, there are disappointments, and after such a strong showing on *You Are Here* the trajectory does not continue upwards. At *best* they have levelled out at a cruising altitude. Whilst the recorded sound is excellent and the production clear and punchy, there is too much mid-tempo ordinariness about many of the songs, and they lack the necessary energy and fire.

The customary UFO traits of power, melody, and dynamics are well to the fore, but some of the material upon which they are deployed is second-rate and lacking in integrity. The fact that Moore's guitars were recorded on a different continent does not bode well for overall quality control. Frequently his inner shredder is allowed more space than is necessary, and, on occasion, his bright, sustained solo tone sounds characterless and processed. The album does have a couple of half-decent rockers, and a pair of classy semi-ballads, but little presented here equals or improves on the promise delivered by its predecessor.

'Hard Being Me' (Way/Moore/Mogg)

Opening with powerful drums, slide guitar, and Mogg's declaration of the band being 'back in town, alright?', a suitably heavy blues riff and a mid-paced Quo-like shuffle kicks in. The verse is a 'boogie-by-numbers' affair with the chorus, 'It's hard being me … I'm dizzy like a monkey on a tree', being marginally better. Moore's solo sounds underpowered and too influenced by modern country blues players, although he still finds a few seconds in which to shred.

Lyrically the song is sub-standard fare although the lines 'I got wounds and cuts, shining like dimes in my eyes' indicates that Mogg hasn't entirely lost his muse. Ending with a repeat of the introductory riff with a harmonica adding interest the song comes to a sudden stop. 'Hard Being Me' is not the impressive opener that was hoped for, but it is, frustratingly, very representative of what *The Monkey Puzzle* has to offer.

'Heavenly Body' (Moore/Mogg)

Parker 're-imagines' the drum introduction of 'Pack It Up And Go' (with added studio trickery), and Way unleashes a massive heavy bass riff which is joined by an aggressively dirty guitar in an excellent mid-tempo funk groove. Mogg's deep, mature tone handles lyrics like 'Burning like a bush fire, sinking in the mire, I trapped her like a birdie, caught her in the wire' with conviction, and the song moves up a gear as a new low-down, swinging riff underpins the chorus.

Moore's solo begins with control and plenty of phrasing to match the groove, but his tendency to over-shred dominates the end of his allotted sixteen bars. 'Heavenly Body' is the best rocker on the album, ending suddenly with Mogg's mysterious recurring lines 'I am changing faces, I guess I'm Mister Hyde'. After the misstep of 'Hard Being Me' this song sounds like the band have rediscovered their *You Are Here* mojo

'Some Other Guy' (Moore/Mogg)

Continuing the bluesy theme established with the first track, 'Some Other Guy' begins with moody keyboard doodlings. A harmonica takes the lead melody over a dull, medium-paced rhythm and predictable chord sequence. Mogg's tone and phrasing of the song's title is impressive and the texture soon heavies up, but it's still a routine chugger with the lyrics detailing the narrator's sadness surveying his empty home now that his partner has left him for someone else.

At 2.38 there's a flicker of musical interest as Moore is allowed space but instead of shining he chooses, for the most part, to shred. It doesn't belong in this style of song. Post-solo, 'Some Other Guy' slopes off home without excitement whilst, left alone in his American studio, Moore unleashes more flurries of notes to the fading end.

'Who's Fooling Who' (Way/Moore/Mogg)

Starting with a steady acoustic guitar rhythm backed by tasteful organ, this is another of Mogg's frequent forays into the world of disintegrating relationships. The chorus is more melodic than the verse both in the vocal line and supporting instrumentation. The rhythm section joins in for the chugging second verse, but again it's all mid-tempo, lyrically uninvolving stuff.

At 2.08 the instrumental is again the most interesting part of the song. There are some long 'violined' guitar notes over a sparse keyboard backing, leading into Moore's solo which is his most convincing work on the album so far. After a final chorus and a brief harmonised solo, there are some pretty repeated short phrases which, with a bit of work, could have segued neatly into the next song.

'Black And Blue' (Raymond/Mogg)

Instead, however, 'Black And Blue' opens with a possibly unintentional homage to AC/DC's 'For Those About To Rock'. This motif is pulverised by Moore and Way's monstrous power-chords and Parker's signature drum rolls, before breaking into a steady, simplistic riff which needs to be at a faster tempo for better effect.

Rising in passion with the lyrics 'He disappeared, fell down the cracks, he walked out never came back' the song moves into an engaging chorus with excellent backing vocals, despite the recycling of two lines from 'Give It Up', 'Lying in the gutter, looking at the stars'. Both lyrically and musically the best moments occur with, 'She was the girl with diamond smile, lost herself on the Golden Mile'.

After another chorus, Moore's solo has some blues, some shred and, best of all, some harmonised melodic lines towards its close. 'Black and Blue' takes too long to finish after its final choruses, with the coda section dragging on for a further unnecessary minute, before hitting an abrupt end with Mogg's unaccompanied, over-enunciated words, 'Baby's in flight'.

'Drink Too Much' (Moore/Mogg)
This is the first-class ballad of the album. Beginning with a stridently melodic guitar line 'Drink Too Much' moves into a mainly acoustic guitar verse which takes a wryly reflective look back on a relationship which has had its share of highs and lows. The bridge and chorus are superb with Moore's short fills, adding much to the song's glorious feel. Mogg is in fine form especially in the second verse, 'Our shadows dancing across the floor, I never wished for, never wanted more, your diamond smile and long black hair, you're much more baby than I ever dared'. Score 50 points in your 'I-Spy Book Of Mogg Lyrics' for a repeated 'diamond smile' in consecutive songs.

After the second chorus, Moore's solo is melodic, carefully phrased and played with real emotion and taste, leading into some excellent fills against further choruses. This is one song which would have been better with a long fade rather than its brief, disappointing coda. This is much more like it.

'World Cruise' (Moore/Mogg)
This, however, isn't. Starting with a bluesy acoustic guitar shuffle, a choir of murmuring Moggs and some overlaid slide guitar fills, this becomes a blues-rock number of the dullest order. Lyrically underwhelming, this tale of a prisoner dreaming of freedom is backed up by a drum machine-style rhythm and a mediocre guitar riff as its very weak spine.

At 2.18 there is a descending run which may have been 'inspired' by a similar phrase in Pink Floyd's 'Money' (it occurs at 3.38,) leading into Moore's solo which he plays with conviction and integrity. It's the only vaguely impressive part of this debacle. The song ends with more acoustic guitar, the Mogg ensemble, and the 'worse-than-Coverdale' line, 'I'm just a whole lotta man, honey'. Are you really? That's nice. Nil points.

'Down By The River' (Moore/Mogg)
'Down By The River' is another 'UFO-by-numbers' song. A predictable chord-based riff sets forth over a medium tempo which lacks energy, with Moore shredding without apparent purpose. Whilst Mogg's lyrics paint pictures, 'It was a blinding light, a sheer tornado of pain, I had a whisky fury, pounding like the Devil's rain', the vocal melody isn't strong, and the chorus is enlivened only by some quality backing vocals.

The instrumental section again holds the most interest (1.52) with a half-time feel, controlled feedback and some slow emotive playing, before a return to the original tempo with Moore delivering familiar-sounding phrases with more than a touch of shred towards its conclusion. There are further choruses before a sudden stop ending to another un-involving track.

'Good Bye You' (Moore/Mogg)
This is the companion number to 'Drink Too Much' and is just as good. Over a steady, staccato rhythm, harmonised guitars sing as Mogg adopts a gentler tone for the verse which sits over a slow grooving rhythm. Lyrically it's not as strong as its sister song, but musically it's got everything that makes a UFO ballad great; melody, harmony, and feel in abundance. The brief bridge is excellent and the chorus even better, with its questioning refrain, 'Is it goodbye you? Is it goodbye me?'

Moore provides some stylish and effective melodic fills in appropriate spaces throughout the song, and his solo is a masterpiece; short, very sweet, and right up there with his best work. The final choruses follow together with a tiny production glitch at 4.23 where the track disappears momentarily. The coda is a short, highly melodic, harmonised section which ends rather than fades. 'Good Bye You' is the last really good song on the album.

'Rolling Man' (Moore/Mogg)
When he's not being the 'Outlaw Man' or a 'Fighting Man' Mogg has a third secret identity. Yes, it can now be revealed ... he is ... 'Rolling Man'. It's UFO for beginners again. Over an uninspiring drum rhythm ('Hey, Mr Parker!'), a sub-AC/DC chord progression settles in for the duration with plenty of woeful words including 'I've got a woman with a magic touch, she's half crazy, she's half Dutch' and 'I've got lightning seeds in my pants, I'm the kind of guy who needs to dance'.

Come solo time Moore rehashes the 'separate riff' idea he used in 'Some Other Guy' before launching into a typical solo which sounds like it was thrown together too quickly. There's a reprise of the opening riff, the third verse mixes lyrics from verses one and two, and the chorus is repeated to a fade. 'Rolling Man' is just another ordinary song, and gives further weight to the argument that just because there's more space on a CD than vinyl doesn't mean you should fill it with forgettable mediocrity like this.

'Kingston Town' (Raymond/Mogg)
'Kingston Town' isn't a big enough song to be the album's closing track. An inverted rain-stick hiss leads into Moore's slightly distorted, arpeggiated chord sequence, and a steady rhythmic drive which lasts until the choruses. The best lines are in the verses, 'This road is winding back, and there's no end in sight, no sign of our dead Lord, to guide us through this starless night', whilst musically the bridge section lurches into a 7/4 time signature, 'And through every open doorway you can choose, and sometimes you win and sometimes you lose'.

The chorus moves into 3/4 time before a return to the bridge as a strummed instrumental section. Moore's effective final solo is played in octaves over the chorus chord progression, and the chorus is repeated with keyboards prominent in the mix. A pleasant harmonised guitar section in the style of Thin Lizzy rounds the song off, but it's a long way from 'Swallow' and, as an album closer, it maintains the strong sense of anticlimax that has been building through much of the record.

The Visitor

Personnel:
Phil Mogg: vocals
Vinnie Moore: guitars
Paul Raymond: keyboards
Andy Parker: drums
Guest musicians:
Peter Pichl: bass
Martina Frank, Melanie Newton, Olaf Senkbell: backing vocals
Recorded at Area 51 Studios, Celle, Germany
Drums recorded at Big House Studios, Hanover, Germany
Guitars recorded at The Core, USA
Keyboards recorded at RMS Studio, South London
Produced, recorded and engineered by Tommy Newton
Engineered by Andy LeVein
Released on the Steamhammer label: June 2009
Highest chart places: US: Did not chart, UK: 99

Following the release of *The Monkey Puzzle* UFO toured extensively for the next two years and then began work on their nineteenth studio album. Pete Way was absent due to persistent health problems resulting from his continuing addictions to drink and drugs, and Peter Pichl, bass player with Nektar, was employed for the album. 2009 was the 40th anniversary of the band and to coincide with the new album UFO hit the road again, this time with Barry Sparks giving an enthusiastic and accurate impersonation of Way's stage persona on bass. When *The Visitor* tour returned to Europe in 2010, Sparks was replaced by Rob De Luca.

CDs were now being issued in cardboard 'digi-pack's and *The Visitor* imitates an old, well-thumbed book, the front cover of which has a framed black and white line illustration depicting a large group of people in poverty-stricken conditions. The impressive artwork and insert is by Tristan Greatrex who would provide album covers for the band for the rest of their studio releases. A colour photograph of the group adorns the rear of the insert booklet which contains all the lyrics in a 'one-song-per-page' format.

Musically *The Visitor* is a *major* disappointment. *The Monkey Puzzle* had been more filler than thriller, but there is little about this third Moore-era offering that stays in the memory. It's disturbing that the band has dropped so far from the high epoch of *You Are Here* to this collection of mostly well-below average time wasters. Whether it's the absence of the rock-centric Way, the increasing dominance of blues playing from Moore, Mogg's homages to his own early blues vocalist heroes, or a combination of all three, this album is far too rooted in American country, blues, and funk genres. There is the occasional cool motif, and an open-sounding production, but *The Visitor* is a long way from the muscular, melodic, and far superior *You Are Here*.

As with *The Monkey Puzzle* there is a lack of passion and genuine energy about the project. It's as if the band were bored of their rock heritage, and wanted to try out pastures new. If Mogg's ambition was to move the band into 'Blues-Land' then he needed far better songs than are presented here. Lyrically there are many references to the United States and Mexico, together with another slew of broken relationship tracks. Moore's familiar, bright sounding overdriven guitar sound, which worked well on both *You Are Here*, and most of *The Monkey Puzzle*, is at odds with the musical styles adopted here. Ironically the best song on the album is a reinterpretation of the title track of Mogg's 2002 side project *Dancing With St. Peter*, and even then Moore's performance is inferior to the original.

'Saving Me' (Moore/Mogg)
The American backdrop is set with a resonator guitar and slide introduction. This is followed by a funky acoustic blues riff and an arpeggiated chord progression with evocative lyrics, 'Some men come from nothing, some men will not bend, some will do the bleeding, till the bitter end'. Subtle bass adds to the atmosphere.

Then the full electric band is unleashed on a heavy version of the opening riff and Mogg sings the same verse again. At the risk of repeating myself, please do more with your talent than simply rehash what we've just heard. Either have some new words or start the song with the heaviness, I don't mind which, but *be more creative*. A more acoustic section leads into a driving chorus with cleaner sounding electric guitars dominating before the low-down and dirty opening riff is repeated. Moore's solo is fast, flashy and works well against the underlying driving rhythm, and a final chorus leads to a sudden stop.

This, however, is not the end of the song as there is a pointless reprise of Moore's solo resonator for a further half minute. This presages some of his egocentric doodlings which would feature on the next album. That said, 'Saving Me' is the best new song on *The Visitor*, it's pretty much downhill all the way from this point on.

'On The Waterfront' (Raymond)
'On The Waterfront' is a well-regarded 1954 Marlon Brando crime film, as well as being the title of this much less impressive song. A light, funk number grooves unspectacularly away over a passive, rolling rhythm whilst a more tuneful bridge section, ('I see trouble coming, I'd watch your back, I see blood-a-running'), has Raymond's organ coming to the fore. In the chorus, Brando is name-checked as he and the narrator are 'skipping stones into the sea'.

Whilst the track is pleasant enough in its own laid-back way, it is almost terminally low on energy and there's nothing about it that will trouble the heart or mind much after it's over. Unfortunately, this rings true for much of the rest of this album. Moore plays a controlled, melodic solo over the chorus chord progression, a brief double-time boogie-feel bridge section moves into a final chorus, and a held chord finish, but it's doubtful anyone is sorry that another song is on the way.

'Hell Driver' (Moore/Mogg)

Luckily 'Hell Driver' has some limited sense of purpose about it. Opening with a simplistic, overdriven guitar riff, Parker gets his cowbell out and sets about the music with some aggression as we enter up-tempo groove territory. The track follows a standard blues-rock chord sequence with Mogg's lyrics being heavily Mexico-centric.

When the song breaks into the bridge section, he turns to begging, 'Oh baby, baby, can I please come home, I've got a pocket of pretty, pretty stones…''. Moore's inevitable solo is … fine. Neither terrible nor brilliant, he unleashes some shred to conclude his contribution before the bridge returns where we learn that the narrator is in jail, 'Here in the darkness, I can feel the rain'. The track fades with Moore throwing in plenty of familiar fills as Mogg riffs alongside him with various words and phrases from the previous four minutes.

'Hell Driver' would never have made it onto *You Are Here*, and would have struggled against the better songs on *The Monkey Puzzle*. Here it's one of the better tracks on the album, which speaks volumes.

'Stop Breaking Down' (Moore/Mogg)

An interesting introduction of heavy power chords reminiscent of 'Give It Up' is thrown away, not to be used again, as yet another mid-tempo rhythm takes hold. 'Stop Breaking Down' is better than what's preceded it as there is greater individual harmonic content which is not reliant upon a standard blues structure. The rhythmic feel is pure Stateside with a chord progression moving above a solid drone in the lower register, and lyrically we are back in the world of broken relationships with both verse and chorus containing plenty of melodic moments.

After the repeated second chorus Moore solos and he seems to have rediscovered his *You Are Here* mojo even if there is the occasional nod towards Van Halen. The final chorus introduces yet-more guitar fills, and the second-best song of the album fades away slowly.

'Rock Ready' (Moore/Mogg)

Hope springs eternal that the vaguely upward curve started by 'Hell Driver' will continue with some much-needed power, energy and integrity. It doesn't. Utilising a virtually clean guitar sound and a slide, Moore conjures up a dull chord rhythm which adds bass and drums into yet another medium speed, bluesy, bar-band number.

More American references litter the lyrics, and whilst the chorus has some sing-a-long elements, the song seems intent on cruising into Dullsville, USA as soon as possible. To aid its passage, Moore produces a clichéd solo with minor moments of shred before a final chorus arrives to finish the number off. Whilst not as irksome as 'World Cruise', 'Rock Ready' has very little going for it, being a well-below-par song even for this album, which is quite some achievement.

'Living Proof' (Moore/Mogg)

A slow descending chord sequence with keyboard backing and a slide guitar melody leads into a steadily pulsing funk rhythm. The verse takes place over the opening chord section, and the chorus features a double-tracked refrain of 'Shake, shake, shake this town'. In the second verse, Mogg takes to repeating himself with the lines 'Cool her up or you can cool her down', from 'Give It Up'. Score 25 'I -Spy' points for spotting repeated phrases from previous albums. Fortunately he is better with 'Murder of crows, the laying on of hands, driving in the dead zone, with no maps or plans', but by and large 'Living Proof' is very average stuff indeed.

A short new section at 2.20 lifts things momentarily, and Moore's under-driven, slide-then-blues solo takes over. It's the best thing on offer here with some tightly melodic phrases and rapid playing towards its end. The song then drifts on with repeated 'Shake's, a slide chorus section, and a welcome staccato, syncopated ending.

'Can't Buy A Thrill' (Moore/Mogg)

Sharing its title, but nothing else as classy, with Steely Dan's debut album, Moore opens the song with another short tribute to Van Halen. Influences quickly put away, a guitar rhythm and steady tempo move us away into another American-style road song.

'Can't Buy A Thrill' may be an ode to Way and his addictions, 'In Peter's land of never-never, exploding stars in space' although Mogg's words are usually open to interpretation. The chorus 'If the girls and drugs don't get you, the liquor surely will', and the second verse 'Photos and paper cuttings adorn the walls and floors, the telephone rings endlessly no one answers anymore', are also good.

After the second chorus, there is a new half-tempo section which increases the heaviness substantially and sounds like the band actually mean it, albeit briefly. This is followed by a short, strange synthesiser effect leading into a busy guitar solo, and a repeat of the chorus. The song chugs itself off to a fade with Raymond's synthesiser filling the gap left by the guitar.

'Forsaken' (Moore/Mogg)

As if this album was not boringly pedestrian enough it is now apparently time to bring the pace and mood down still further with a ballad. Worryingly similar to 'Back Into My Life', this slow-paced, tired-sounding country number is yet another failed relationship saga where Mogg's voice is stronger than his lyrics.

Searching for positives, which is tough going, there are some effective backing vocal 'ooohs' in the pre-chorus chord progression, Moore does a good impression of a country guitar picker, the bridge section ups the energy level slightly, and Raymond's tasteful keyboards add interest. Then it's solo time. This is an under-powered stroll through familiar Moore phrasings followed by another bridge and chorus, and you start to realise you could die peacefully in your sleep listening to this musical equivalent of Mogodon.

'Forsaken' comes to an actual end rather than a fade, which is unexpected but nothing special, like the track itself. A half-hearted round of dutiful applause would follow were this song to be played live.

'Villains & Thieves' (Raymond)
Starting with a straightforward, repetitive, two-chord overdriven riff, this mildly promising introduction soon descends into yet another tedious blues-rock number, admittedly with some heavier guitar sounds. Raymond mixes honky-tonk piano and organ into this impersonation of later period Status Quo. Mogg quickly bores with his repeated 'money's and 'honey's and although the chorus is better, his phrasing of its final line, 'Mama's playing a tune on my guitar', fails to fall in with the number of beats rest available.

The bridge is odd both musically and lyrically as the story diverts to a new character, Semprini, an informer who is 'going to go down the pan'. Moore then introduces a slower grinding riff which leads into his solo which just about touches the ceiling of adequate, and then repeated choruses lead to a clichéd rock ending. There is a disproportionate amount of reverb applied to Parker's final bass-drum fill, without apparent purpose.

'Stranger In Town' (Barth/Parker)
An intriguing spiralling guitar and organ riff starts off this dirty sounding funk-based groover with its Mafia styled lyrics. Mogg's tale of revenge fuelled with bitterness sounds suitably brutal, and whilst the lyrics border on the banal at times, for instance 'If the fish don't eat you, oh the money will, if I don't beat you, someone will', there is at least some inherent power in this song. Melodically the section at 1.36 ('Everybody's at the party'), is an improvement with an emphasis on energy.

The instrumental features some tasteful interplay between Raymond's fills and Moore's long, sustained notes before the guitar solo, which does its job satisfactorily, no more, no less. A reprise of the 'Party' section moves into a musical break lifted straight from 1970s prog-rock with power-chords underpinning organ runs which build to a sudden ending.

'Dancing With St. Peter' (Mogg/Kolman/Galaas)
Bizarrely Mogg chooses to cover his own song, the definitive version being on the $ign Of 4 album. Listen to the original with Kolman's sublime playing, and compare it to Moore's phrasing and fills which are allowed to take up too much space in what should be a relatively empty soundscape.

This regretful ballad is the best song on the album by dint of it being written mostly by other musicians. Mogg's best lines of the album are here, 'So don't tell yourself you're misunderstood, 'cos underneath we're all damaged goods'. Unbelievably he manages to trip over himself in the phrasing to the soaring bridge, 'There's a star in the bright sky, some supernova'.

As audition songs go 'Dancing With St. Peter' shows, Kolman would have been a far better guitar fit for Mogg at this stage of UFO's career. Equally, it would have been fascinating to hear Laurence Archer or Paul Chapman's takes on the track. Moore needs to control his tendency to shred when apparently bored as such self-indulgence does this high-quality ballad no favours. The track meanders away to an inconsequential conclusion, which is an appropriate epitaph for the entire album.

Seven Deadly

Personnel:
Phil Mogg: vocals
Vinnie Moore: guitars
Paul Raymond: keyboards, rhythm guitars
Andy Parker: drums
Guest musicians:
Alexa Wild, Marino Carlini: backing vocals
Lars Lehmann: bass
Marc Hothan: harmonica
Produced, recorded and mixed by Tommy Newton at Area 51 Studios, Celle, Germany
All guitars by Vinnie Moore recorded at The Core, USA
Keyboards and Raymond's rhythm guitars recorded by Andy LeVien at RMS Studio, South London, and Steve Ward at SW Sounds
Released on the Steamhammer label: February 2012
Highest chart places: US: Did not chart, UK: 63

The overall impression of 2009's *The Visitor* was one of overtly American blues, country and funk styles supporting largely lacklustre songs. Compared to the sublime, muscular *You Are Here* it seemed that UFO was once again intent on turning into a flimsy State-side shadow of their once-mighty selves.

By 2010 it was clear that Pete Way's addiction-damaged health was not going to improve sufficiently for him to remain a member of the band and consequently a difficult decision had to be taken. Way would never write, record, or tour with UFO again and when work began on the new album, Lars Lehmann was employed as the band's (temporary) bassist.

Hopes were not therefore high when *Seven Deadly* finally emerged. Way's absence from *The Visitor* had signalled a possible permanent loss of hard rock direction and, upon hearing this extremely variable collection, that fear was not dissipated.

The striking, colourful cover artwork depicts a skeleton partially dressed as a cowboy standing at the gates of an overgrown Mexican graveyard. Inside the digipack is a colour group photo with three of the band laughing, Moore alone looks like he doesn't get the joke. The CD booklet continues the overall look with the song lyrics and a list of the band's other releases for the record label.

Seven Deadly is an annoying entry in the UFO canon. It starts with genuine promise; the first three songs are fine examples of excellent melodic hard rock, and there's a superb blues-flavoured ballad. But then the album quickly goes into a tailspin and becomes just as disappointing as its perplexing predecessor.

The recorded sound is again powerfully punchy and clear, and Mogg's mature vocals are reliably strong, but it's the paucity of really good songs that once again lets the side(s) down. Moore's signature overdriven guitar tone is at odds with much of the material presented here and, whilst Raymond and Parker acquit themselves well, the sum is not greater than its parts. For those fans who hoped that *The Visitor* was a one-off aberration and that the band would come to their rocking musical senses, *Seven Deadly* remains a savage kick to the ears, and not in a good way. The diminishing returns curve remained in place.

'Fight Night' (Raymond/Mogg)

Who knew that Paul Raymond was an AC/DC fan? Opening with a riff that would bring a wry smile to Angus Young's face, this rocking number is the best album opener since 'When Daylight Goes To Town'. Mogg's gift for melody lifts the basic, satisfying groove from what could be predictable to a higher level, although he has developed a penchant for humming along with the music before a verse begins.

There is a melodic, quieter, half-tempo mid-section after the second chorus which features subtle slide guitar in the background. Reverting to full volume Moore's employs an underpowered overdriven sound for his blues-meets-shred solo over the verse chord progression, before moving into more melodic phrases which work well. There are two further choruses before the song slows to a clichéd ending, of which Angus would surely approve.

'Wonderland' (Moore/Mogg)

Moore has clearly been listening to the Chapman-era albums for inspiration. The opening and tempo of 'Wonderland' basically plagiarises the magnificent 'We Belong to The Night' riff. Fast, tight, and full of energy, this is UFO back to their committed hard-rocking selves. Effective, slide guitar supports the verse vocals, and when it's time for the solo Moore takes advantage of the song's pace to unleash his shredding powers to great effect. He produces better melodic lines over the chorus chord sequence, and then everything disappears leaving just the riff and an echoed whammy bar scoop.

The powerful rhythm kicks in again, leading to the chorus, and an entirely new and too brief coda section which could have been the basis of an interesting song in its own right. On the debit side 'Wonderland' lasts longer than it needs to, but it's still a welcome inclusion and hopefully indicative of even better things to come.

'Mojo Town' (Moore/Mogg)

And come they do. A magnificently powerful funk riff is the formidable foundation for this slow, rhythmically intense song. Blues and funk are mixed into the heaviness which drops down in volume for the verses. It's a sensational, brooding groove which builds in power to the superb chorus, 'Going on down, going down, going down to Mojo Town', with excellent backing vocals, and Mogg's voice rebounding back and forth in the stereo separation.

Moore introduces a savage new riff at 2.03, which sounds like mid-Seventies Black Sabbath, and another one which is just as brutal and twisty at 2.31.

His solo is suitably squealy, slow, and expressive, with space left in-between phrases, where shred is kept to a tasteful level. This leads into a reprise of the first pre-chorus and chorus sections, followed by the return of the 'Sabbath' riff bringing the song to a sudden aggressive ending. At just under four minutes 'Mojo Town' isn't long enough, it conveys power, melody, conviction, and intensity, and is deserving of further development. Three tracks in and things are definitely good.

'Angel Station' (Moore/Mogg)
Using an E-Bow, (a small electronic handheld device which causes a guitar string to vibrate indefinitely), and subtle delays, Moore's smooth introduction over gently strummed acoustic chords with sustained keyboards support Mogg's evocative opening phrases, 'I spent twenty years of walking, eighteen years of talking, one year to lose you, five of regret'. 'Angel Station' concerns the death of a loved one, and the inevitable practicalities that follow bereavement. This is an unusual subject for a rock song and it receives a sensitive emotive treatment.

A steady rhythm grooves away under the main body of this track with a familiar Moore melody appearing with the words 'And this don't come easy, nothing comes for free'. This is followed by an effective clean-sounding chord-riff section before the second verse, which is, irritatingly, a virtual retread of the first. The chorus is excellent, again ably supported by the backing vocals, and leading into the third verse with tightly picked guitar arpeggios working well with the lyrics, 'On the beach, we found a bottle, the message read within, mother you were beautiful, that was your only sin…'. Moore's lengthy solo is expressive and tasteful, moving into the concluding chorus. The coda is a reprise of the opening stanzas and brings this highly effective ballad to a slow, considered conclusion.

'Year Of The Gun' (Raymond/Mogg)
And that's it for the good songs – it's heavy going all the way from here. 'Year Of The Gun' features a dry, clean country-style guitar riff and another steady, pulsing bass and drum rhythm. There is a slight increase in interest at 0.54 as the song lifts musically and lyrically, 'There's no mercy under the miracle bell, glamour and glitz, God's fiery hell, the underbelly that heroes can't move, in the night time rush that bubbles and brews', and its companion section at 2.15.

This is a tale of gangland violence and retribution and is familiar territory for what is fundamentally a dull stroll through a blues flavoured song. Moore's solo breaks out over Parker's heavy tribal drum rhythms before reverting to the opening riff and repeated 'Year of the Gun's as the number finally makes its tired way to an end.

'The Last Stone Rider' (Moore/Mogg)
Opening with some shimmering guitar chords, 'The Last Stone Rider' quickly becomes another medium tempo number with a major chord riff sequence. Mogg's vocal melody is strong although the song itself, as with its predecessor,

sounds like a leftover from the sessions which led to *The Visitor*. Backing vocals enhance an unexciting chorus and, at 2.10, a new, darker, funky riff enters the fray. This leads Moore into his part-bluesy, part-melodic, part-flashy solo, although much of his phrasing sounds overly familiar having been used frequently on past records. A final chorus leads into a different chord section which acts as a brief coda to this uneventful track.

'Steal Yourself' (Moore/Mogg)

'Steal Yourself' begins with another under-driven introductory chord progression, this one suggestive of 'Owner Of A Lonely Heart' by Yes. It is supported by more mid-tempo dullness, which perpetuates the fear that the band has lapsed back permanently to *Visitor* levels of dissatisfaction. This track is almost a direct continuation of 'The Last Stone Rider' and feels sluggish, the guitar arpeggios under the verse being similar to Whitesnake's 'Ain't No Love In The Heart Of The City'. The chorus is a little better melodically, 'And you steal yourself for one of those highs again, kill yourself for just one lie', but Moore's solo again fails to engage emotionally. After a repeat of the chorus, and some time-wasting guitar doodles, the song appears to come to an unspectacular end at 3.41.

Except it doesn't, weirdly restarting with just guitar and vocals before the rhythm section joins in. Moore then proceeds to perform one of the worst guitar outros in the history of recorded music, fiddling around with a short atonal phrase that won't quite work no matter how many times he attempts it, which is in excess of 20. The song goes into a fade as an act of self-preservation probably out of sheer desperation with Moore's playing.

'Burn Your House Down' (Moore/Mogg)

And worse is to come. This slow, overly long, rhythmic ballad has laid-back guitars and subtle keyboards playing a very ordinary chord sequence, which even the backing vocals can't save. 'Burn Your House Down' is stronger lyrically than musically, but then again it was bound to be, 'There's a sunset close behind, there's a blue light calling me, trouble of the heart tonight, I'm so blinded I can't see', and 'Sometimes I take out this gun, alone on Ocean Boulevard I put it in my mouth and play out my final card'.

But it's another disappointing relationship song, with nobody except Mogg sounding like they are particularly bothered about what's going on. Fortunately, Moore's contribution is emotive, and even if it's tied down by his often-used phrases, it's still the best section of the song. 'Burn Your House Down' is yet another track which sounds like it belongs on *The Visitor*, where it wouldn't have been thought of favourably either.

'The Fear' (Moore/Mogg)

Three consecutive albums, three consecutive dire mid-tempo shuffly blues rock songs; 'World Cruise', 'Rock Ready' and now this abomination. Thanks.

It is beyond reason why these massively clichéd, completely predictable, and intensely unrewarding songs are allowed space on UFO albums.

One of Mogg's final couplets is 'I got the fear now, gimme a beer now'. Seriously? Is that the best you can do? The song ends in exactly the way your average pub band would finish it. Well done everyone.

'Waving Goodbye' (Moore/Mogg)

'Waving Goodbye' is, appropriately, the last half-decent track on the album, opening with some strong strumming and an effective guitar melody. The mood lightens into a gospel-style verse, with Raymond's organ well to the fore. Lyrically Mogg could be criticising Schenker although, as with much of his poetic word-smithery, this is open to interpretation. The texture is heavier for the chorus with high-quality backing vocals.

After the second chorus, there is a reprise of the introduction, which builds into a long guitar solo featuring plenty of screaming notes, and melodious phrasing. A repeated chorus section is full of instrumentation and power, and leads into a quieter, predominately acoustic, regret-filled coda, 'Lost everything, but nothing was mine, and I'm saying goodbye for the very last time'. And at this point the album should have ended, enough being enough. However...

'Other Men's Wives' (Moore/Mogg)

Hiding behind a complete misrepresentation of the words 'bonus tracks' on the front cover of the CD booklet is this unpolished 'gem'. If I wanted crud like this I'd buy late period Quo which is just as pointless, frustrating and under-achieving. It's only a bonus if you consider what you receive to be of worth.

This conviction-lite impersonation of ZZ Top is a medium-paced shuffle without distinguishing features, and a terrible, terrible chorus, 'I caught my baby with another man, I'm gonna kill him because I can, shot him dead right between the eyes, you don't mess with other men's wives'. Married to a man with this sort of personality defect perhaps the woman in question decided to make the first move. Maybe she'd listened to this album and realised that almost anything was better. You can see her point of view. *Seven Deadly* is well named. Out of eleven tracks, so far seven of them are indeed deadly. Deadly dull.

'Bag O' Blues' (Raymond/Mogg)

Another song with an interesting interpretation of the word 'bonus', 'Bag O' Blues' opens with the sound of a stylus hitting a vinyl record, and an aged piano tone. This slow number is the only song in UFO's recording history to feature just keyboard and vocals. Mogg appears to be paying homage to early blues songs of his youth by writing one of his own.

Taken in isolation, it's pretty enough, with Raymond playing some effective lines, but putting it on a UFO album, *a UFO album*, even one as ultimately disappointing as this, is seriously questionable. At the end of the song, and the album, we hear the needle leave the vinyl groove, probably in despair.

A Conspiracy Of Stars

Personnel:
Phil Mogg: vocals
Vinnie Moore: guitars
Paul Raymond: keyboards, rhythm guitar on 'The Real Deal', backing vocals
Rob De Luca: bass
Andy Parker: drums
Recorded, produced and mixed by Chris Tsangarides at Ecology Room Studio, England.
Mastered by Helge Engelje
Guitars recorded at The Core, USA
Released on the SPV/Steamhammer label: February 2015
Highest chart places: US: Did not chart, UK: 53

Continuing the three-year gap between albums, 2015 saw the release of the final collection of original songs by UFO. Touring bassist Rob De Luca was promoted to a permanent member and contributed to two songs on the album. Further change was afoot with the relocation of the majority of the recording work back to England under the watchful eye of legendary rock producer Chris Tsangarides, who was well regarded for his work with Thin Lizzy and Judas Priest, amongst many others.

Sound-wise Tsangarides opts for a somewhat softer mid-range, less overdriven guitar tone compared to the tighter, brighter mix of the previous four albums. Parker's drums sound suitably strong whilst De Luca growls away effectively at the bottom end. Raymond's keyboards add significantly to the texture without smothering the overall feel, and Mogg's mature vocals are like a high-quality brandy, smooth with depth and bite. Lyrically he remains his usual elusive self, but at least this time we aren't being treated to a virtual travelogue of the United States and Mexico.

Overall there is a welcome move away from the 'Americana' sound which dominated *The Visitor*, and which was a substantial feature of *Seven Deadly*. The new album is closer in feel to *The Monkey Puzzle* and *You Are Here*, but what lets *Conspiracy* down is, again, the absence of consistently good songs. There are some moments of greatness, some glorious riffs, and excellent instrumental moments, but too many of the tracks lack sparks of genuine inspiration. Especially in the latter half of the album it feels like whatever was put forward for consideration received approval.

Noticeable by its absence is a ballad of the quality of 'Swallow', or 'Drink Too Much'. One factor that has always marked UFO out as a superior band is their ability to write slower songs with similar emotional heft to their rockier output. There is nothing on *Conspiracy* which fulfils this role, and the album is the lesser as a result.

The CD booklet cover is a magnificent melange image of a functioning underwater city complete with a sunken ship and operational U-Boat. This dreamlike quality continues inside with numerous similarly classy images, and the song lyrics. The inlay also documents all the albums of the Moore era but dispenses with any pictures of the band.

The version of *Conspiracy* released to the Japanese market included an additional track, 'King Of The Hill', which is a rollicking rocker in 12/8 time. It is stronger than over two-thirds of the material presented on the rest of the album. Mogg is in excellent voice, Raymond's organ supports this high energy number, and Moore supplies an excellent, fast solo.

Conspiracy is, in effect, UFO's signing off album, although at the time Mogg had not announced his decision to leave the band. Their final studio album, the all cover version *The Salentino Cuts*, was yet to come, but this still leaves *Conspiracy* as only an equal third-best offering of the band's final period. The first four songs of *Seven Deadly* are far superior to virtually everything on this album, and yet *Conspiracy* doesn't have the terribly slack quality of the remainder of the songs of its immediate predecessor. *Seven Deadly* starts off by shining brilliantly. In comparison, *Conspiracy* is a permanently lit ten watt bulb.

Since the cornucopia of riches that was *You Are Here* UFO has consistently struggled to keep the quality of their songwriting at such 'dizzy, dizzy heights'. The departure of Pete Way had clearly left a significant rock shaped hole in the band, with too many so-so songs and uninspiring playing taking his place. *Conspiracy* does what it does with some small degree of success but, as a final original flight, it feels very average, leaving much more to be desired than it delivers.

'The Killing Kind' (De Luca/Mogg)

Saving the finest till first, 'The Killing Kind' opens with an overdriven guitar riff around which Parker thumps his drums into submission before adopting a familiar tempo for this upbeat rocker. De Luca's rumbling bass and Raymond's subtle organ are well placed in the mix as Mogg sings over an AC/DC style chord progression. The bridge is better than the verse, and the chorus is memorable, uplifting, and glorious.

After a repeat of the verse/bridge/chorus structure, the song heads off into instrumental territory for the rest of its duration. Moore is good here with a well-structured, melodic, unshreddy solo. Raymond's organ is brought closer to the foreground, and some two-handed guitar tapping takes the song into a fade. This is a fine example of the band at their latter-day best.

'Run Boy Run' (Moore/Mogg)

Another chord based riff groover with the cruise control set to medium, Mogg's sardonic lyrics 'Mr Cocksure, Mr Changeface, first in the trough and fix the race' and 'So Mr Junkie, oh Mrs Tramp, where'd you leave your moral stamp?' are the strongest elements of this ordinary little rocker. Devoid of dynamic contrast, 'Run Boy Run' doesn't really grab the attention until the instrumental section at 2.18.

Suddenly a spacious soundscape opens up with a quieter funky guitar riff and atmospheric chords. Moore's solo begins with slide and then grows from bluesy phrasing into many, many shredding clichés in a four-square pattern. After the final choruses, part of the central riff is repeated three times bringing the song to an end. Moore, however, fails to take the hint and continues to widdle away pointlessly for a few more seconds.

'Ballad Of The Left Hand Gun' (Moore/Mogg)

A ballad in the sense of historical storytelling, 'The Left Hand Gun' is also the title of a 1958 film starring Paul Newman as the cowboy Billy The Kid who was (incorrectly) depicted as being left-handed. Knowing Mogg's fondness for outlaws and guns this may have had some bearing on his writing. Initially the ghost of *The Visitor* raises its unwelcome head with a resonator playing a shuffled rhythmic introduction which is joined by bass and powerful drums. Fortunately the track manages to save itself by adding a reasonably heavy funky blues riff, and the chorus ups the melody quotient.

In the second verse Mogg sings some of the worst lines he has ever written, 'I have a clock up on the wall, comes from China, don't tell the time at all, women came and women went, some were ugly and some heaven sent'. Mogg has a great sense of humour, especially on stage, but there doesn't need to be an attempted example of it on record.

At 2.28 there's another interesting ethereal instrumental as Moore plays isolated phrases against a slow power-chord backing. This moves into another tasty funk-based riff at 2.57, before the solo proper is played out over the chorus chord sequence finishing with a brief harmonised passage. Further choruses lead back to a reprise of the resonator and slide introduction, and a sudden end.

'Sugar Cane' (Moore/Mogg)

Sustained keyboards are broken up by attacking drums, soon settling into another under-paced chord sequence with a suitably low-slung funky riff. An unspectacular verse leads into a better chorus, 'Fall, she's the colour of rain, my sugar cane'. Lyrically this is another of Mogg's outlaw scenarios, but it is Moore's solo which commands the most attention, even though he walks through musical territory he has ploughed more than once in his UFO career.

There is a repeat of the chorus followed by a coda section lasting nearly a minute and a half, which is a weird amalgam of reduced dynamics, synthesiser, and some hazy meanderings around the guitar fretboard. It's unnecessary, and the song hasn't been interesting enough to warrant this extension.

'Devil's In The Detail' (Moore/Mogg)

Borrowing part of its opening riff from the chorus progression of 'The Killing Kind' speaks either to the quality of the former or a lack of inspiration here. Moore solos over the mid-tempo chugginess that ensues. Whilst backing vocals lift the chorus, its central idea, 'The devil's in the detail' as part of a couplet, is then rehashed a further unnecessary five times. Twice would suffice.

Lyrically Mogg may be reflecting back on the excesses of UFO at the height of their popularity, 'The gates of Babylon opened, we fell upon our prey, everything was taken, it was the summer of our day'. There is some subtle interplay between guitar and bass at 2.58 which leads into another excellent riff at 3.16 with shades of a slightly slower 'Mother Mary', until the main solo kicks in begins with the blues and builds to a shreddy conclusion. Another chorus leads to the song's end but not for Moore! He proceeds to contribute another twelve seconds of completely unnecessary and meaningless flash phrases. Yes, Vinnie, we all know you can play...

'Precious Cargo' (Moore/Mogg)

Another subtle shuffle rhythm with prominent bass and keyboards sets this lengthy track off. Moore provides ghostly, sustained notes before the restrained verse under which some U2-style delayed arpeggios are introduced. There is a heavier, commercial sounding build to the chorus which, again, is uninspiring but has at least got some power behind it. Lyrically the second verse is good, 'The truth is stacked in this deck of cards, a promise lost wrapped in these ivory barbs, Elizabeth sings oh she's my queen of hearts, souls of men die and actors pick up the parts'.

The long instrumental section reprises the introduction, and the words 'jam' and 'session' spring to mind as Mogg murmurs, and Moore noodles away. The volume leaps up for repeated choruses, and the coda section again features the introduction. This is the third time we've heard this and it wasn't great the second time around.

At 5.25 the song finishes, but Moore doesn't, playing away to himself for a pointless further twenty-five seconds. Vinnie! Go to your room, think about what you've just done, and only come downstairs when you've got some decent riffs and solo ideas.

'The Real Deal' (Raymond/Mogg)

Fading in with a slow drum rhythm there is a palpable sense of boredom on the horizon and, sure enough, an unexciting chord progression with De Luca prominent in the mix duly unfolds. Every aspect of this song is dreary, underpowered, and uninvolving. The chorus goes on for twice its natural length, and the only time ears may prick up is in the bridge section, 'And we said goodbye to the morning and the falling sky, the meanest year we ever saw, before we said goodbye, goodbye'. There is no solo section, the song coming to an unusual end after Mogg's repeated exhortations that this is 'the real deal'. It isn't. Or, if it is, I want my money back.

'One And Only' (De Luca/Mogg)

An energetic and confident-sounding introduction is cut short by a typical American rock sequence (chords changing over a steady single bass note drone,) over which Mogg's lyrics are brought in on autopilot. Moving quickly into a good-time-blues-rock style chorus, the cliché-quota is met with the line 'It ain't over till it's over', but luckily 'it ain't over yet'.

After a further verse and chorus Moore solos over a different chord progression and, whilst being typically and instantly identifiable as him, it is still the most involving element of this song. At times very high pitched and shreddy his contribution is nevertheless melodic and magnificent in comparison to the music it's set in. A predictable rerun of the chorus leads to the song's close.

'Messiah Of Love' (Moore/Mogg)

Another standard funk-rock number, Mogg's declaration of love is not up there with his finest work, although fans of predictable rhymes will be delighted with 'Let me take you to heaven above, let me give you the Messiah of Love'. The bridge section, 'Some come to do battle..' is the most stimulating part of the song, followed by a brief bluesy solo, and a repeat of this album's 'Big Idea' - the atmospheric instrumental section.

On 'Messiah of Love' this occurs at 2.40 with bass and guitar playing off each other. Another strong funk riff appears at 3.10 with greater levels of guitar overdrive, over which Moore unloads another typical solo. Inevitably there is a repeat of the chorus before a sudden ending.

'Rollin' Rollin'' (Moore/Mogg)

Anyone hoping for a closing track to match the quality of the opener is going to be disappointed. Another mid-paced riff blends guitar, bass and organ effectively as the song moves into a quieter, possibly autobiographical lyric, 'I was a high roller, tightly wound, never missed a beat, never had my feet on the ground'. This leads into a heavy funk riff and a tired sounding chorus. The next verse is better, 'All the dry drunks gnash and wail, they all have such a scintillating tale, it's a cold wind blows through the pines, up from the coast to the Death Valley Line'.

Never one to let a good musical idea go unrepeated Moore unleashes the 'Quiet Bit' yet again, this time at 3.03 with guitar, bass and keyboards all contributing interesting fragments. Then the inevitable solo arrives, followed by further flashery getting in the way of Mogg's final vocals. Either would be fine at this point, but not both.

Repeats of the chorus lead to a reprise of the quieter instrumental section with Raymond's keyboards adding to the fading atmosphere. 'Rollin' Rollin'' is no better or worse than all the other average tracks on *Conspiracy*, and that is as damning as it is disappointing.

The Salentino Cuts

Personnel:
Phil Mogg: vocals
Vinnie Moore: guitars
Paul Raymond: keyboards, backing vocals
Rob De Luca: bass
Andy Parker: drums
Instrumental recordings at Big House Studios, Hanover, Germany
Engineer: Mirko Hofmann.
Vocal recordings and album mix at Ecology Room Studios, Kent, England.
Engineer: Chris Tsangarides.
All guitars recorded at The Core, USA.
Album mastering by Helge Engelke
Produced by UFO
Released on Cleopatra Records: September 2017
Highest chart places: Did not chart

There are eight cover versions dotted sporadically through UFO's back catalogue. 'Peak cover' was achieved on *UFO1* where three numbers were non-originals but, given the poor quality of the group's compositions at the time, this was actually a benefit. *Phenomenon, No Heavy Petting* and *Lights Out* served up one disposable track apiece. *No Place To Run* gave us the sterling 'Mystery Train', and *Mechanix*, the awful rendition of 'Something Else'. Since 1982 no UFO album had included anyone else's songs, so it came as a surprise to learn that the band's next album would be a collection of other artists' work and, in retrospect, their studio swansong.

The words 'contractual' and 'obligation' hang over *The Salentino Cuts* like a middle-aged letch in a nightclub. It's far quicker, and therefore cheaper, to re-work existing songs than go through the labours of producing a whole album's worth of new material. If this was the case then, taking into account Mogg's awareness of the physical demands of touring, the decision to 'pay homage to a dozen of their personal favourites' (as the sticker on the front of the CD case proclaimed), seemed an easy way out. The choices are puzzling as it is well documented that Mogg's early musical heroes include Jack Bruce and Howling Wolf, neither of whose work features here. Just a thought.

The cover artwork depicts a jukebox surrounded by some indistinct photographs. The album title itself is a curiosity. Salentino is a dialect spoken in a part of Sicily. How does that fact fit with this collection? Perhaps the words just sounded good together. The CD booklet continues the jukebox theme with information on the songs, together with a group photo. This features Mogg taking a sort-of-bow front and centre, with the rest of the band standing moodily behind him. The singer's pose may be a subtle indication of his decision to stand down.

A much more appropriate sign-off would have been a live album with performances recorded on the 'Last Orders' tour as a fitting conclusion to a band who have always viewed themselves as being at their best on stage. A double live CD could feature performances from the late Paul Raymond and his familiar replacement Neil Carter.

Or we could have had the current line-up playing songs from UFO's distant past. It would have been interesting to hear Raymond's influence on anything prior to *Lights Out,* and Moore's take on older songs ('Boogie' and 'Prince Kajuku', for example), would have been intriguing. Also the stronger songs on *Misdemeanor* have always deserved a second chance at a better life. This type of project would have been a fascinating 'full circle' rounding off of the band's career.

As a further alternative they could have gone down the 'unplugged' route and developed purely acoustic arrangements of some of their classics. Any of these ideas would have made a worthier farewell, and be infinitely preferable, to what was eventually foisted on fans.

Instead we've got this dubious collection of updates of some well-known and some obscure songs, and what a pointless exercise it is. However, in a desperate search for something positive to say about this lacklustre mixture, Mogg's voice is, as ever, nothing short of expressive, and occasionally he is a preferable listen to the original vocalist. Moore, when he stops short of shredding and actually plays an appropriate solo, fits in well with these modern re-imaginings. Raymond's contribution is both subtle and substantial, and Parker and De Luca sound like they had fun recording these songs. It isn't, however, a lot of fun to listen to and, after a couple of plays, *The Salentino Cuts* sat on a shelf, gathering dust.

'Heartful Of Soul' (Gouldman)
Graham Gouldman, who would go on to be a member of art-rock pop band 10cc, wrote this song for The Yardbirds. Here his quaint, dated pop number is given a rocky re-working which adds grit and muscle to the intrinsic melodies, especially in the chorus where the 'Lights Out' rhythm again grooves away powerfully. Dispensing with the original's backing vocals in the chorus Mogg is in fine voice, and Moore's relatively restrained solo brings a fresh and modern feel to the track.

'Break On Through (To The Other Side)' (Morrison/Krieger/Densmore/Manzarek)
Driven by some sprightly drumming, this is a spirited rendition of the clichéd late Sixties sound of The Doors' 1967 'classic'. This version has a decent energy and tempo about it, and an interesting guitar riff under the title's words. Raymond's take on the solo section is historically accurate, but the 'correct' absence of an actual guitar solo leaves this cover in an unremarkable and pointless state. An instrumental duet between keyboards and guitar

would have been an interesting development; however slavish copying seems to have been the order of the day.

'River Of Deceit' (Martin/McCready/Baker-Saunders/Staley)

This slow, restrained country-style ballad by American band Mad Season is an unlikely choice, and a new song to me. The UFO version adds little to the atmosphere of the 1995 original beyond the low pitch and maturity of Mogg's vocals, and Moore's effective playing, especially in the closing section. The melodic lift into the chorus is effective, but the overall feel is of hypnotically sparse, emotionally intense, navel-gazing.

'The Pusher' (Axton)

Released in 1968, Steppenwolf's savage indictment of drug dealers is given a steady-paced and occasionally heavy reworking with muscly, overdriven guitar. Organ and bass feature clearly in the mix, and Mogg is especially poignant with the repeated refrain 'Goddamn – the pusher man'. Moore spends too much time meandering around the fretboard during the verses, and it would have been intriguing to hear the more inventive and tasteful playing of Jeff Kolman.

'Paper In Fire' (Mellencamp)

John Mellencamp's mid-Eighties song effectively blended rock rhythms and instrumentation with subtle banjo and acoustic guitar to produce a spacious, powerful recording. Much of that subtlety is lost in UFO's markedly rockier and slightly faster remake. Again Moore is overplaying and needs to leave more space between phrases for his contribution to be musically persuasive. De Luca's throbbing bass propels the song along effectively with some occasionally interesting motifs thrown in.

'Rock Candy' (Hagar/Montrose/Church/Carmassi)

Montrose and UFO were both gracing rock's stages during the early 1970s. This is a very meaty take on the under-recorded blues-rock original. Mogg's vocals are preferable to those of Sammy Hagar and he sounds spectacularly lascivious on the repeated 'hot, sweet, sticky's in the chorus. There are no keyboards in the song, and their inclusion would have given this update a more modern, identifiable edge, vocals notwithstanding. Thankfully Moore stays mainly true to the slow, menacing solo of original guitarist Ronnie Montrose, particularly in the rising octave section towards the end of the instrumental.

'Mississippi Queen' (West/Laing/Pappalardi/Rea)

Parker's cowbell and a suitably heavy guitar and bass riff make for a slow blues-rock groove in this highly similar homage to one of Mountain's standout songs. Again Mogg's voice wins out but, whilst the recorded sound is superior to that of 47 years ago, there is really nothing else particularly distinctive to separate the new from the old. Some keyboards in the mix would have been a useful sonic addition to provide contrast in the arrangement.

'Ain't No Sunshine' (Withers)
This classic soulful ballad, originally written and sung by Bill Withers, is badly damaged by Moore's persistent guitar fills. It would have been better to restrict the initial instrumentation to acoustic guitar, subtle percussion and bass. For this version to have had real merit full use should also have been made of Raymond' creative keyboard skills, rather than have him merely replicating the string sounds of the original.

Moore could have opted for a subtle acoustic solo or a clean electric sound which would have improved things no end. However, once again, he turns to his brightly overdriven guitar tone to which some delay effects are added to dominate the soundscape, turning the song into an overly busy, bluesy mess. 'Ain't No Sunshine' is the perfect song for Mogg's voice to shine in, which it duly does, but less Moore here would definitely have been preferable.

'Honey Bee' (Petty)
Tom Petty's excellent 1994 album *Wildflowers* is a wide-ranging affair, with 'Honey Bee' being one of its rockier tracks. UFO's version is at a slightly faster tempo, and with a heavier sound. However, Petty sang his songs better than anyone else, and this glossy rock makeover doesn't really work on any level. Moore's contribution is sonically unwelcome again, especially in the final chorus sections where he is all over the place most of the time. Compare and contrast this with long-term Petty guitarist Mike Campbell's tasteful and well thought out phrasing and again the thought occurs, 'What would Kolman play?'

'Too Rolling Stoned' (Trower)
Bridge Of Sighs was a breakthrough album for Robin Trower, and 'Too Rolling Stoned' is one of its more famous songs. Trower is a huge fan of Jimi Hendrix and Moore manages to be respectful of this with his initial heavily wah-wah'd contributions. As with the original, the song changes into a slow 6/8 time blues shuffle just past the half-way point during which Moore gets on the solo train again. Fortunately, he restricts himself to staying in the wah-wah-blues corner of the carriage rather than filling the available two-plus minutes with relentless, unyielding, flashy shred.

'Just Got Paid' (Gibbons/Beard/Ham)
An aggressive drum and guitar introduction give the ZZ Top song a heavier lease on life with some effective slide guitar fills. Mogg sounds particularly at ease with this funky blues-rock classic but, beyond his vocals, nothing is that much different or better than what was released back in 1972. Moore shows

himself adept at doing a decent impersonation of Billy Gibbons but, as the original wasn't broken…

'It's My Life' (Atkins/D'Errico)
The final track is very similar in feel and sound to 'Heartful Of Soul', especially with Raymond's prominent organ. Whereas Gouldman's song had plenty of bounce and melody in its stride, this is a much more leaden affair. The best part is the refrain 'It's my life, I'll do what I want', but it takes what seems like a long time getting there. The coda section has Mogg singing against himself and adding an unintentionally comic sounding 'Don't push me'. There's an interesting funky guitar riff in the background during the fade, but overall this is a dull rendition of a dull song by The Animals. It's a poor closer to an unspectacular, unrewarding, and unnecessary album.

Thank You And Goodnight

As I write this UFO is back on the road with their farewell 'Last Orders' 50th Anniversary tour. My last encounter with the band was at Rock City in Nottingham in March 2019, and shortly afterwards the shock news of Paul Raymond's death from a sudden heart attack broke. An integral member (on and off) since July 1976, the 73-year-old's keyboard, guitar, and songwriting contributions to the band were substantial.

Determined not to let this unexpected tragedy prevent them from saying goodbye to their fans, UFO contacted Neil Carter who resumed the role he had undertaken in the early Eighties. Mobile phone footage uploaded to 'YouTube' shows Carter throwing himself into his work with unfettered enthusiasm, and those fans who remember his original contributions are only too happy to see him back in action.

In contrast, the near soporific stage persona of bass guitarist Rob De Luca is a disappointment. For all his faults Pete Way was the beating heart of UFO, and his now sadly permanent absence leaves a void that cannot be filled. Way returned to the stage recently with The Pete Way Band playing a mixture of self-penned and some classic UFO songs in small venues. If you wanted to see a true definition of pathos, his shows provided it.

Way wore his heart on his sleeve, but the abuse he had put his body through showed all too plainly. He no longer played the bass live, restricting himself to the unlikely role of endearing frontman and, inevitably, his singing skills didn't match those of his former band-mate but, as he said, 'We're doing our best'. Way died in Bournemouth on 14th August 2020, a few days past his 69th birthday, after suffering a serious injury at his home two months earlier. His 2017 autobiography *A Fast Ride Out Of Here – Confessions of Rock's Most Dangerous Man* is an entertaining, no-holds-barred read which throws much light onto the rock'n'roll lifestyle he and the band enjoyed in their heyday and afterwards. A natural showman Way is credited with influencing many rock bassists in look, style, and attitude, if not technical musical dexterity, and his death was another unnecessary shockwave to the history of the band in their final years.

Michael Schenker, meanwhile, continues to issue recordings and tour, currently with his 'Michael Schenker Fest' gigs which feature most of the vocalists who have sung with, and been sacked by, him over his long solo career. Although Schenker has spent more time out of UFO than in, his name will always be associated with some of the band's greatest songs and, arguably, their best creative period, a point he acknowledges by continuing to include several UFO numbers in his setlists.

The band's other major guitar contributor, Paul Chapman, never managed to match Schenker's draw as a solo artist. A member of 'Waysted' between 1984 and 1987, he subsequently played with several different groups, including American southern rockers Gator Country, and more recently Killer Bee. Until his sudden and untimely death on June 9th 2020 (his 66th birthday) he was teaching guitar from his home studio in Melbourne, Florida.

Whilst the 'Last Orders' tour is Mogg's farewell to both band and fans, he has given his blessing to UFO continuing without him. This seems as unlikely as it would be unwise. Mogg's unique vocal and lyrical contributions cannot be matched and, if the band decides to carry on without him, they will, in effect, become their own tribute act, forever compared to past glories with nothing new or special to communicate. It's a brave – or foolish – person who takes his place.

There are numerous 'Best of UFO' compilations available, all of which, by and large, tread the same musical ground. Never one to miss an opportunity, Chrysalis Records issued a further collection to coincide with the final tour. Appropriately titled *Last Man Standing* it contains exactly what the seasoned UFO watcher would expect, and already possess. The collection does not feature any post-*Misdemeanor* songs, the last album the band recorded for the label. It, therefore, misses out on three decades of music, not all of it great, but certainly none of which should be ignored.

Beyond the official live albums referenced earlier, there are two excellent box sets: *UFO At The BBC 1974-1985* is a six-disc extravaganza featuring concerts from 1974, 1975, 1977, 1980, 1982, and 1985, together with a DVD of television appearances between 1979 and 1982. The *Official Bootleg Box Set 1975-1982,* is another multi-disc package of gigs recorded in 1975, 1976, 1977, 1978, 1981 and 1982. Hopefully, there will be a commemorative double live album of the final tour, their first since *Showtime* back in 2005. This would be a much better farewell than Chrysalis's predictable money-grabbing, bandwagon-jumping strategy.

If you're a CD rack browser and want the 'best of the best' albums from each significant era of the band, (Schenker, Chapman, and Moore), then *Obsession*, *The Wild...*, and *You Are Here* should be in your hands. Three to leave behind from the same periods are, without question, *Sharks, Mechanix,* and *The Visitor.* Every self-respecting rock fan needs a copy of *Strangers In The Night*. It should be a law or something.

If you're a digital play-list compiler and want a deeper dive into a 'best of' the band try taking one track from each album. My selection, avoiding the obvious and going for the less well known but still satisfying songs would be:

'C'mon Everybody'
'Prince Kajuku'
'Time On My Hands'
'Out In The Streets'
'Reasons Love'
'Try Me'
'Pack It Up And Go'
'Anyday'
'Long Gone'
'We Belong To The Night'
'Diesel In The Dust'

'Heavens Gate'
'Between A Rock And A Hard Place'
'Ain't Life Sweet'
'Pushed To The Limit'
'Midnight Train'
'Perfect View'
'Black Cold Coffee'
'Drink Too Much'
'Saving Me'
'Mojo Town'
'The Killing Kind'
'Heartful Of Soul'

If life was fair UFO would be up with the true giants of rock music, being mentioned in the same breath as Zeppelin, Sabbath, or Rush, and deserving of similar levels of commercial success. But, blessed with a seemingly effortless ability to shoot themselves in their collective feet when on the brink of such acclaim, they managed to relegate themselves to outright winners of the 'Best Band That Should Have Been Huge Award'.

Changes of key personnel, unwise choice of producers, unnecessary changes in musical direction, excessive alcohol and substance abuse, and bad timing, all contributed to this situation. It remains true that whatever success and acclaim UFO has achieved, it could and should have been so much more. They are publicly endorsed by stadium-filling acts such as Iron Maiden, Metallica, and Guns 'n' Roses, all of whom count themselves as fans.

The UFO legacy will be one of timeless, classy rock songs, crafted with power and melody as their backbones. When they were at their best, they were unmatchable. When they (infrequently) disappointed, they were the musical equivalent of socks on Christmas morning. Whilst their live performances have become as much the stuff of legend as the off-stage japes and shenanigans, what UFO has always been deadly serious about is their music. In the long run it's the songs that truly matter, and with a back catalogue of genuine rock classics, it is their unique musical contribution that places them right at the top of rock's branches.

It's been quite a ride this last half-century!